Boat

to

Baguette

HETTIE ASHWIN

Published by Slipperygrip 2020
Boat to Baguette: Copyright
© Hettie Ashwin

PAPERBACK
ISBN: 13 978154275634 published 2017
POCKET EDITION
ISBN: 9782956686842

Illustrations by Hettie Ashwin

www.hettieashwin.blogspot.com
facebook.com/alacrity.vivacity

Books by Hettie Ashwin

<u>Humour</u>
Literary Licence
The Reluctant Messiah
Mr Tripp buys a lifestyle
Barney's Test
The Truffle War
Fat Bits
Murder! Mayhem! and lesser cuts of meat.
I'd rather glue me nut sack to a bullet train

<u>Thrillers</u>
The Crowing of the Beast

<u>Short Stories</u>
After the Rains & other Stories
A shilling on the Bar

<u>Speculative Fiction</u>
Pi Trilogy
The Mask of Deceit

<u>Novellas</u>
A Strange kind of Paradise (series)

Nothing is more
difficult,
and therefore,
more precious,
than to be able to decide.

Napoleon Bonaparte

DIKERA

1

We are never bereft of a bright idea.

We are schemers. We often, when there is nothing much to do, lie back and plan, plot, and ponder on the vagaries of our life. It keeps us on our toes.

My husband and I have the added advantage of a totally over-the-top positive attitude that makes things happen, so it was no surprise to us when we decided to just 'up sticks' and buy a boat to sail the world.

Of course, the boating lifestyle was a big change. We had to sell our household furniture, send the kids for medical experiments and willingly throw all our money at the idea. But it was a plan.

Our idea was to sail away into the sunset and see the world without the benefit of Airbnb, hotels or a tour guide. It wasn't so much a hippy lifestyle as a shippy one. We would be self-sufficient, free of traffic, jobs and having fun.

There is a small bone of contention on who saw our dream first. I maintain I found the yacht on the internet, Boomie says he saw it first. The thing we agreed upon, it was just what we wanted. We didn't exactly go into the deal blind, because we had purchased another yacht previously with the grand idea to 'fix-it-up-a-bit'. These words translated into 3 years of learning about sand blasting, welding, painting, scraping, swearing, moving house to accommodate a 44 ft boat in the backyard that needed to be put there by a 100-tonne crane and quite a few dollars. We soon found out that having a dream and paying for it were two separate issues.

The 'Red Boat', as it was affectionately known in times of humour, was our baptism into just how much a good idea at the time might cost and how much of that time it will suck from your life. Of course, being the eternal optimists, we didn't see a problem in craning a bloody big boat into our newly acquired back yard so we could work on it at our leisure. Not that we actually had any leisure. Between kids, work and normal living we squeezed the boat into our lives. It wasn't called 'Magic' by the previous owners for nothing.

All good things come to an end, thank heavens, and after looking at that big beamy red arse out of the kitchen window for a few years we decided that someone else might like a little magic in their sadly lacking lives.

The Red Boat wanted water, not a back yard, and so we admitted defeat and sold her to someone with a bit more passion for the fixer-upper.

We did lament – for about a month – because you can't just drop that much money into a dream and not do a bit of lamenting, but we took a collective deep breath and moved on with our lives. I vaguely recall Boomie giving me a high five as the new owner trucked the thing away, but hey, life is full of ups and downs.

They say that the two happiest days of boat ownership are the day you buy and the day you sell. That's pretty much on the money…or lack thereof.

Naturally the rather large learning curve we vaulted over on the Red Boat would hold us in good stead if we *ever* went looking for another. Not that we were looking exactly, but you know how it goes. I can only equate it to childbirth. At the time it isn't much fun and you swear you will follow the Chinese model of only one. But by the time you get home, put the kettle on and sit down, it wasn't so bad after all.

So, before we knew it those fateful words once again passed our lips.

'No harm in just looking.'

That 'look' came at a price we could afford. Obviously, we didn't want to repeat the mistakes of the Red Boat so we studiously told each other that this one ticked all the boxes. Given the right conditions you can convince yourself that the moon is made of cheese.

This one felt right.

The logistics of 'upping sticks' was to sell the family home. You can't go travelling the world and still be thinking about the reticulation system and electricity bills. It had to be all or nothing.

And there is nothing like having 3 garage sales and seeing your goods go to strangers to really feel like you are progressing in the dream stakes. Boomie sold the kitchen table while I was having lunch on it, such was his fervour for the sale. We divested ourselves of our worldly goods like they didn't matter. I packed all my books and sent them to a foster home for the duration. There is a limit to my largess to strangers. You just never know what life will bring and maybe one day I might be able to be reunited with my little darlings. Downsizing my Tupperware was as liberating as going braless after a hard day in the garden.

With all our worldly goods on the boat we moved on-board and began to dream of grand adventures. I don't know about you, but I have always felt the world was there to discover. Nothing was too far, too dangerous or too hard. With our dream firmly in our sights there were just a few wee little itsy-bitsy bits of the boat that we wanted to just make our own mark. Just a bit of this and that. Not much really.

Nothing comes without a few alterations. Things to make it yours. It might be fluffy dice on the rear-view mirror or in our case a bit of a re-fit.

The phrase so often used in boat building- well a couple actually are:
The person who built this wasn't a shipwright's #@&hole.
*Why did they do that for Christ's sake?
*I don't know what they were thinking.
And the one that crops up over and over,
*How much did you say it costs?

We practiced all of them to varying degrees as we made our boat our home. I bought books. I read books. We made plans for every eventuality and eventually we set a date.

Well, things never go quite as smoothly as one

wishes. That date went by and many more took its place as life took various turns. Boomie always said it was for a reason. That pragmatic view has oftentimes been our get out of gaol card.

'It's not in the plan,' he'd say. It was a convenient, yet somehow quite valid answer. In the meantime, we both retired and went sailing and had fun. We were living the dream, albeit in Australian waters.

And then we found an exotic pest.

Not your everyday pest, but a wood eating pest. The man from the Environment Department said,

'I think it's exotic.'

'What do you suggest?'

His glib answer was to 'just strip the timber out.'

I have never seen Boomie shudder inwardly, but we knew what was coming. I think I actually gasped. It was the Red Boat all over again. Even the eternal optimist can have an off day.

The only thing to keep the dream alive was to drink red wine and take a deep breath. Several wines and breaths later,

'How hard could it be?' I mean, we had cut our teeth on the Red Boat. We knew the pitfalls, the time involved, the money – oh the money. But on the plus side we were in Port Douglas, far north Queensland. It wasn't such a bad place to be. People called it a tropical paradise. All those tourists can't be wrong.

The work began, and we bought half of

Bunnings – and had the biggest love affair with a hardware chain store since Mills & Boon.

And this is where our story really begins.

2

Why not think big.

On an off day when pulling the boat apart and putting it back together again made the excite-0-meter bottom at zero, Boomie was reading the paper – the editorial to be precise. Boomie, and to a lesser degree myself are political animals. We discuss, we rail, we talk about, and generally roll our eyes skyward in distain at the state of the nation – any nation.

This particular day a fellow distainee had written in to the editorial, (that last bastion of free speech) to say as the nation goes to hell in a handbasket he had retreated to France, where civilization still existed. Where the living is easy, birds are singing and cotton is high.

And it got ol' Boomie thinking.

If ever there was a dangerous man, it is a man with an idea…and the internet at his disposal.

Why is it we are in Australia?

Why is it this boat takes all our hard-earned money?

Why is it we are dissatisfied with our lot?

These questions rattled around the boat for a few weeks. A few weeks to brood, pout just a little and ponder. I couldn't answer his queries off the top of my head. They were big questions that required big thinking. The Ashwins are good at big thinking. We do our best thinking in the *big* style. I made a list of answers, but none had that spark of ingenuity, uniqueness or homespun sense. Not that we hated the boat. That didn't seem to be the issue. We loved the boating life. We just didn't like the way she took all our money and our time for the promise of something in the future. We needed a goal. Something we could sink our hearts into that didn't involve a trip to Bunnings, the hardware store. We felt adrift.

I should point out that our ponderings had been going on for some time. For a few years we had been thinking about where we would like to live out our remaining days. There would come a time when we couldn't swing our leg over the gunwale anymore and the most we can pull is the skin off a rice pudding, so starting an outboard would be out of the question.

I am a great believer in planning ahead. Sometimes the plan is only five minutes ahead of the execution, but it's good to know there was a plan just the same.

We had toyed with the idea of finally swallowing the anchor – as they say in nautical terms – somewhere affordable, welcoming and not too hot. Twenty odd years in the northern part of Australia in tropical paradise with skin cancer, mozzies, sand-flies and other creepy crawlies that come in 4 metre lengths and have sharp teeth, is enough.

Not that we hadn't had fun. We had been

doing what we loved to do. Our passages had been exciting, interesting and we'd met some quite entertaining people. We'd weathered storms, sailed into the sunset, anchored off leper colonies of old and caught just one large barramundi. Life was full of challenges, laughs and the odd cringe-worthy moments.

In shopping around for our retirement excitement, I had read about many places.

Malaysia have a grey hair policy. Show them a healthy bank balance and they welcome you with open arms. Indonesia is the land of smiles and Aussie bar culture. Asia was cheap living we had heard. Sailors on the dock love to talk about the fabulous $5.00 meals and the endless summer. But everyone knows you can convince yourself into and out of anything with enough red wine… or champagne. Asia wasn't for us. We wanted something a bit further from the equator. Somewhere where a jumper/pullover doesn't look out of place. Somewhere where we understood the culture.

The thought of France came to us like an idea we had been waiting for all our lives.

I had done the Europe trip in my wild youth plus a few other destinations. Europe was full of good things. Europe was a veritable smorgasbord of things to do and it had four seasons, not two. That alone made us think on the possibilities. Boomie had also been overseas, so it wasn't like we were stepping off into the unknown.

The boat took a back seat as we had a break from the refit and I regaled Boomie on my French experiences.

I had cycled in France in the late '70s and all my memories were pleasant ones. Well apart from the time I had to politely eat tripe. Ghhhhhhhwwwhhh. Still makes me shudder.

I remembered a French farmer taking my girlfriend and I in for the night. His wife was horrified that two young girls should sleep in a tent on their field. We were treated like royalty, albeit with a bit of oddity thrown in. The next day, loaded up with baguettes, jam, fruit and tomatoes we were waved off by the whole family as if we were going to the wilds of Borneo never to be seen in polite company again. This scenario was played out to varying degrees throughout my travels. But the French held the record for congeniality.

I heard about Boomie's travels and the amazing bottle of red in a tiny café in Calais for about the price of a box of matches. Clearly France had made a favourable impression in the 1970s. Although, 40 or more years later, the appreciation of good food, good wine and friendly natives surely could be considered constants in this ever-changing world. We hoped so.

By jingo I love the internet. Being a planner and one who makes lists, the internet furnished my fertile imagination with any number of variables. Boomie only had to plant the small kernel of the idea that Europe was our final destination and I took that thought and ran with it.

The internet is the go to for everything these days. I love the way you can get an answer to any question you might dream up. I dreamt up some pretty knotty questions regarding our new adventure.

There are forums for expat sprouting all over the World Wide Web. And it looked like they all had something to say. I found out how to get a good paint job in Portugal. How to register a car in Russia and how to go about living in another country. As anyone who has done a bit of 'research' on the internet will know, one soon becomes an expert … of sorts. I trawled the forums for the good news and the bad news regarding France. I could tell straight away that some people would never be satisfied unless they had a little bit of home in a foreign land. The word immerse entered my vocabulary as I became an expat snob. No fish and chip hunt for me. No hording Lipton tea bags, we would dive right in and *immerse* ourselves. Forums are all very well for the newly minted expert, but what I wanted was answers to my particular circumstances. The way I saw it we were breaking new ground here, and maybe virgin territory.

My first big question that seemed the most obvious was, will France want us?

I knew we were fine upstanding citizens without criminal records. I knew we paid our bills on time. I knew about three French words.

Of course, one needs to be pragmatic about these things. With all the turmoil in the world these days and the movement of whole populations across the oceans it could be a little harder than one imagined to move to another country no matter how big your bank account.

In a moment of pure genius, we thought we could just sail there and arrive by boat and claim asylum. Asylum from what in Australia we weren't quite sure, but knowing the Ashwins we'd think of something. There could be humanitarian grounds. Australia just doesn't have the red wine we like and the French do wine so well. And I'm sure I look good in a beret.

When asking questions, I prefer to go to the horse's mouth. Rumours, theories and hearsay are all very well for the women's magazines, but there is nothing like getting the facts…which incidentally can then be relayed to the husband as if I'm an expert. Who doesn't like garnering brownie points from your nearest and dearest? I emailed the French consulate with a lovely worded letter. I started with *Bonjour* and ended with *Cordialement*, but the guts of the email was in English. Surely the French Consulate in Sydney would read English. I pressed send with high hopes.

One thing Boomie and I do is scenarialize. We talk over the likely outcomes of everything from getting a letter back from the consulate in Sydney to getting out of a hostage situation in the Red Sea. It keeps us fresh.

Vis-à-vis the hostage situation, I always maintain no-one would want the Ashwins without our life-giving drugs, taken once a day. Without them we'd be useless.
'Come with me if you want to live.'
'Hang on a minute, just get my tablets.'
Mohammed might urge Boomie to walk faster, but without his gout pills the entreaty would fall on

deaf ears. Which by the way he has from years of motorcycling.

'Eh?'

The hostage takers would try to wake me up to get going, but with my thyroid pills somewhere else my fatigue would be debilitating.

And you can imagine their response when we say,

'Have you got any sun-cream, 'cause we'll only last five minutes in the sun without it?' We'd get a medal for the most annoying hostages in the world. Of course, they could just shoot us and to be honest without our pills, that might be the best option for all concerned.

We thought about what the consulate might say and planned our lives in response.

The other thing I did was look at France in the atlas. It's best to get your head around what the country actually looks like in great detail if you are going to live there.

'Been to Paris yet?'

'Huh? Where's that?'

There is a certain rush I get from knowing that I could, given the right circumstances, live wherever I choose. Why stick to your own back yard when the world awaits. It is a measure of true freedom and daring-do.

You know how it goes. 'Went to Mogadishu last Easter for a short break. Loved it. Thinking of buying an apartment.' 'Ever been to Sierra Leone? You know you can bring your own gun!' 'France? Why not?'

France is quite big for a European country and full of towns, villages and city centres. The different districts take in the Mediterranean and the Alps, the Atlantic and the English Channel. Sharing borders with Switzerland, Italy, Germany, Belgium and Spain it sits in a perfect place for travel. If you have ever been surrounded by choice you will know what we faced. Picking a place to live just because you like wearing boots, scarves and hats isn't very scientific. Choosing a location because it's near 24-hour motorcycle racing at La Mans has merit, but I preferred the shopping experience of Paris to racing.

With a little bit of compromise, we decided with modern high speed trains and motorways that have 130 km/h limits nothing is very far.

'Pfffffht. In Australia we travel 300km for a loaf of bread for lunch.' The tyranny of distance held no fear for two intrepid Australians. For heaven's sake in 300km we could be eating croissants before 10am.

'They'd be chocolate croissants of course,' Boomie said.

'*Mais bien sûr*.' (But of course).

3

Bucket lists come in all sizes.

Our bucket list began to grow as we fed ourselves a diet of historic sites, food and wine festivals and must-see architecture; not forgetting that Venice would be only a hop skip and jump away. We hadn't quite got around to looking at property, but such was our enthusiasm, we were already thinking house swaps to Venice, Vienna and Vancouver.

Boomie had always had an interest in WWI sites. They went on the list. We toured France while reclining on our bed in Port Douglas. I wanted to go to a mushroom festival in Provence and taste truffles.

'Put it on the list.'

He wanted to see Amiens Cathedral.

'Put it on the list.'

I had a hankering to see the prehistoric monuments of Brittany. Carnac with its megaliths and tumulus burial grounds.

'Put it on the list.' You can see where we were headed. Straight into scenarializing our way to la la land. We hadn't even had a response from the consulate on one measly lousy question. Just a *oui* or *non* would have sufficed.

Then Boomie said those fateful words.

'No harm in looking.' These words should come with a warning and terms and conditions in fine print.

'This is how it always starts,' I said.

And so it did.

'Let's not get carried away,' he said. I nodded

'We need to see what we can afford,' he said. I nodded.

'We could go to the Isle of Man TT motorcycle races you know.' I nodded.

Of course, looking at real estate in another county, a country that has chateaux, castles, estates and Paris is just tempting fate. I mean, the word chateau is enough to give a sparkle to your eye. Here is the definition just to put you in the picture.

A **château** is a manor house or residence of the lord of the manor or a country house of nobility or gentry, with or without fortifications.

Don't all stories start in a chateau and end up with happy ever after? It was enough to give me the willies. The word excited doesn't quite cover it. They say you shouldn't believe all you read on the internet, but looking at French real estate was real in the extreme.

The boat languished in Port. We were still working on it, but not with the enthusiasm of old. The wet season had just kicked in and the heat and humidity were draining our meagre reserves for work. There was a change in the air.

I'm not one to sit still and so I began to

16

bookmark some real estate sites for further study. The methodical thing to do was to sort the list of houses into districts.

The web pages make it all so easy. Districts are clickable on a map. Prices are sorted from high to low or the other way around depending on how big you want to dream. Two bedrooms? Garage? Half a vineyard? A truffle farm? – Now you're talking.

'You're getting carried away Hettie,' he said.

'Look, I found a castle within spitting distance from a marina.' He started to take an interest. 'It has a gun turret.'

This was more fun than cutting plywood. Whittling down the list was hard work. Passing judgement on people's furniture was a doddle.

Right here, I must say, I never knew that French people had a fascination with wallpaper and particularly ugly light fittings. Perhaps I had lived in the tropics for too long and my tastes leaned towards magnolia paint and rattan furniture. Some interior shots I looked at were time pieces from the 1970s. Some people had no idea about the principle of this goes with that. I mean, who in their right mind would put brown tiles with red rose flock striped wallpaper?

What you need to do is look beyond the tat, the hideous décor, the ghastly lace curtains and the cringe worthy light fittings and use a bit of imagination. Lucky for me I was good at envisaging and scenarializing the innards of the houses. The liberating thought about the whole thing was that we didn't possess any furniture. There was never that moment of angst trying to see if Granny's dresser would fit through the door. We had nothing to begin our household experience. Some houses came with a bit of furniture. Although, by the look of the pictures, all you needed was a winter's day and a box of matches to start the homemaking process. Some adverts said we could keep the fireplace. That's a comforting thought. Some fixer-uppers came *sans* (without) roof. Was the roof extra?

It quickly became apparent that parts of France were in the desirable areas, others came under the heading of 'only if you must'. The latter, of course, were the cheaper seats.

Anything with a decent amount of sunshine, a pool or within sniffing distance of the Mediterranean was expensive. If you want to rub shoulders with the elite you'd need to pay for the privilege. We decided we didn't need to hobnob. If we wanted a hot summer, then we'd need to go back to work and pay top dollar for the experience of getting sun stroke. The tropics had cured my lust for palm trees, so I looked more north. The Alps would be cool. A cool million or so. The Alps were in a Euro league of their own.

A weather map on the internet is a grand device. It gives you the average rainfall, temperatures and the like for any country you care to mention. Not that I was looking to find a quiet spot in Southern Sudan, but you know how the computer can suck you in, and before you know it, you are absorbing useless facts like alcohol at hen's night.

In France there was quite a difference, I found, between the south and the north. The North had the seasons we were looking for. The North had cheaper properties.

'Paris is in the north,' I said.

'So is Amiens,' Boomie said.

I began to look at Normandy. It sounded dependable, and something we could pronounce, and being near the UK, if we wanted tea bags, we could just jolly well go and get them. I began to scout around the environs of Normandy when Brittany popped up. Another district we could pronounce, bonus.

All I could confidently say about Brittany was that I'd heard of it and didn't they have a bit of a seafaring background. And I recollected the Bretons wear striped shirts. On closer research the Bretons were descendants of the Britons of Cornwall. I began to look in Brittany. It was a focus that fuelled my imagination.

Brittany is a bit of a forgotten piece of France. It has always been treated as the 'other' bit, sticking, as it does, on the north-west corner out into the Atlantic Ocean. It's not very big, but has a history all its own. And the icing on the cake for me was that as I applied the filters on the real estate web pages, time and again Brittany came up as the cheapest place to buy property. Perhaps it was the back of beyond and no one wanted to live there. Or perhaps it was the best kept secret.

There was one house that fired our desires. We called it the German house. It was a solid looking townhouse, three stories high, built on a corner. The attraction of this property was that it hadn't been mucked about with in any way. Everything as far as the agent was concerned was original. The pictures bore this out. The oak staircase was a dream. The ancient tiles on the floor looked like they had been there forever, but it was the history that enthralled. The Germans had occupied the top floor in the war. That floor had its own staircase from the street and its windows commanded a good view. I visited this house a hundred times on the internet, dreaming of polishing the wood around the windows and doors, and cooking in the big ol' French provincial kitchen with a fireplace and one of those drying racks hanging from the ceiling. The German house was our benchmark. The only thing it didn't have was a garage. Could we perhaps rent one somewhere else? Could we squeeze one in downstairs? I kept looking.

Here I was, looking at houses, moving furniture around, pretending we were living there, and I hadn't received a reply from the French Consulate regarding our eligibility. It was all a bit premature, but it was still better than painting two pack paint and shopping at the hardware store.

Once again as I searched for houses I became
an expert at navigating the real estate speak.
Spin doctors are the same the world over. Cute
meant pokey. Rustic meant it was falling down. A
renovator's dream – well we all know what that
means. Doing all this looking I began to refine our
needs versus wants. We had lived on the boat for
11

Do we really need a turret?

years with one forward berth, a galley, a bathroom and a saloon in 13.5mt. Did we really need two bathrooms, five bedrooms and a loft conversion?

'I think I can survive without a sunroom.'

'Do we really need a turret?'

'Shall we have with, or without fortifications?'

'What about a moat? I'm not sure I can do without a moat.' We culled our list to bare essentials. What we wanted was small(ish) home with a garage…'cause a man's gotta have a shed'. And a roof would be nice.

4

It is all in the detail.

With still no answer from the Consulate I decided to dig a little deeper into the whys and wherefores of our French adventure. I tried to ring. Naturally, the answering machine was in French. I pressed *quatre* and left a message after the tone.

It was apparent to me that if we were going to go to France then I needed to read the fine print. House hunting took a back seat. The boat was on a go slow as the tropical summer began to take hold of our enthusiasm, and I felt I assumed the life of an internet spy as I roamed all over the consulate site and the forums for expats.

This research quickly made me feel a little inadequate.

The French Consulate work in a rarefied atmosphere and don't deal with the public. For a proletariat country they looked like they didn't get their hands dirty with the hoi-poloi. I realised my phone message would be sucked into a vacuum. I devoured the web site and learned,

The Consulate staff will not answer personal queries. Refer to the web site.

The Consulate staff will not respond to emails if the answer can be found on the web site.

The Consulate have a two-hour lunch.

Welcome to the first step of French bureaucracy.

I like a challenge. Game on!

The Consulate, for the uninitiated, is a quagmire of do's and don'ts. The main thing they are interested in is paperwork, and you do all the work.

We needed copies by three of just about our whole life story and so I began a file. Just to make sure, we copied everything and then had them certified by a J.P. with a rubber stamp on every piece of paper. What could possibly go wrong?

The police check was simple enough. All you needed to do was hand over the money and fill in the form, an occurrence that would become all too familiar.

We waited with baited breath to find out if we had hit the Interpol top ten.

We needed a letter from the bank to say 'Yes, this is the bank account of Hettie Ashwin.'

We needed 3 month's worth of bank statements. They wanted our income and outgoings. They needed our health insurance documents. There was a request for our flight tickets, our house documents…house docs?

We hadn't bought one yet.

'So,' Boomie said, 'I guess we should go and look.' You don't need to ask me twice if I want to go to Paris- I mean France, and look at houses. It was all becoming a reality.

'We don't need to buy anything. We are only looking.'

'I know. I know.' I said.

'And if nothing else we will get away from the

boating lifestyle for a bit.' A change is as good as a holiday they say.

'It could be a holiday,' I said. 'Absolutely no pressure.'

The biggest conundrum was the ol' catch 22. We needed permanent residency to buy a house. It seemed fool hardy to embark on a house purchase without knowing if we would be allowed, or be desirable enough for the French Government. It was obvious that we needed to live there, but to get permanent residency we needed a house. It was the chicken and the egg.

Anyway, we were only looking. And if by some miraculous chance we found something and by some sheer luck we bought it – well how could the French refuse two fresh faced innocents like us. It would be a punt. It just might be the gamble we were willing to make.

Of course, you can't just rock up on the real estate door step and ask for the keys to a house. There are steps to be taken. I took steps.

First, we made a list of the houses we quite liked and I emailed the agents to say we would like to view. Did I say how much I like the internet? Within a week or so I had answers to all my queries. The best part was everyone replied in English. I guess when you have money to spend it ups the stakes and even speaking Icelandic wouldn't be too much trouble.

Now the tricky part started. We wanted to maximise our time and our hire car and so we bought a rather large map from the newsagents and plotted an itinerary that would get us at point A at 9:30 and then point B at 3pm and then on to C, D, and E. Naturally nothing would get done between the hours of 12 and 2. Lunch!

As our trip began to take shape and our airline tickets booked, the next thing to do was to co-ordinate the agent's appointments. There was quite a bit of emailing as I made plans. It felt a bit like a Napoleonic campaign. A few weeks of planning and we had most of our 17 days covered in appointments. Then came the Airbnb part of the puzzle.

Airbnb is fabulous It's cheap, you meet some amazing people and get to stay in all sorts of places. It was exciting to tie up all the ends and in about three weeks our trip was planned and paid in full, courtesy of Mr Visa and some pretty serious saving. I began to love 40 fishfingers for $4.00. All for a good cause.

I had allowed for a few days at the end to go south and see some boaty friends, so it wasn't all 'work'. That part of the trip was the 'just wing it'. With the Ipad and free wifi all over the place I could book Airbnb on the fly. It sure beats ringing around and in faulting French trying to get a room A lot had changed since I was travelling in 1978. All for the better.

This was our first-time o/s for ages, well years and as the time drew near we threw ourselves into the trip, all the while trying to temper our enthusiasm with phrases like,

'We don't need to buy anything.' 'We are

just looking.' 'At the very least we'll have had a holiday.' All this was trumped by, 'We are friggin' going to buy a house in France!'

A hard one to beat.

5

Travel is an education.

If I had the money I would travel first class or better still, have my own jet. Travelling cattle class isn't much fun no matter what the brochures say. It's cramped. It's uncomfortable and why we always get the coughing maniac and the seat recliner is beyond the statistics of averages. The only good thing is the movies, which make time fly – especially if, like us, you don't watch movies or have a television. I catch up on all the block busters. And I read a bit as well. All you can really say about long haul flights is 'Thank God it's over.'

Travelling half way around the world is bound to put your body clock out of whack. We were running on empty when we hit Charles De Gaul airport. Luckily all my meticulous planning kicked in and we entered the real world with our eyes wide open. Feeling like hicks we marvelled at the soldiers, the people, the bright lights, the people, traffic and the people. Port Douglas felt like the back of beyond compared to CDG airport. We were now living in the fast lane.

One of our first introductions to the modern age was negotiating a McDonalds hamburger joint. We had never seen a pick and pay and collect before – in

French. You look at an interactive touch screen and select your poison. Then you pay with your card, get a ticket and wait for your number to be called…. in French. I rehearsed what my number would be when called. First French lesson negotiated to satisfaction.

Paris is modern, Paris is multicultural. Paris is Paris.

'I don't think we are in Kansas anymore Toto!'

Next step was picking up the hire car.

We had packed light so our one case would fit in a small car. I had asked for the cheapest small car available. At the desk we were advised that for just a few Euro extra we could go up one notch. We went up. We had a modern French Renault Clio. I'm absolutely hopeless with cars. Spotting one in a car park is a nightmare as they all look the same. I tried to commit this Clio to memory. The last thing you want is to try to put your key into another car.

The woman behind the counter gave us what looked like a credit card and sent us on our way into the cold March morning. Boomie still had sandals on and he was a bit underdressed at 2 degrees.

As we walked to the car park I said,

'We don't have a key.' We wondered if there was a concierge somewhere who would help. We trundled about looking for the Clio with the number plate to match our documents and eventually found it. I know new cars can have keyless entry, I have watched a few movies to glean that much, but after stowing our stuff in the boot we couldn't seem to get the car going. I went in search of help. Without a key I just couldn't see how we were to start the

28

thing. Boomie waited around and tried to find a handbook.

Our old ute in Port Douglas was devoid of electrics. We had wind up and down windows, one key and that was it. This Clio was all the bells and whistles. I found a fellow who really didn't have any idea either. So we didn't feel such idiots knowing I had collected one more human who didn't have a clue. Boomie had a brain wave as we hunted around for the credit card thingo to go somewhere. Turns out it goes in the centre console. There isn't a 'key' slot on the column at all. Who'd have thunk it?

No one wants to look like an idiot on their first day out and so I sent the other idiot away and we tried to figure out how to make the engine go. There was a start button, but when pressed it just popped out again.

'Perhaps the car was made for fail safe idiots,' I said. Boomie tried pressing the button while putting the car in park with his foot on the brake. …ah … idiot proofing wins again. Everyone wants to save you from yourself.

Of course, starting the car is only the first step. We now had to get out of Paris in the morning peak hour (or three hours) of traffic on the wrong side of the road with only a road map bought in Cairns to lead the way – piece of cake. It only took three attempts to get out of the car park – good start – then we were merging and hitting the ring road.

I had studied the road via the internet, but nothing prepares you for the mental agility needed to negotiate the roads at warp speed. It was dangerously thrilling. The trick is to keep calm.

Boomie followed my instructions and we were on our way with just one mistake that took us to a dodgy looking back area that might have doubled for a movie about drugs, trafficking of children and car-jacking. I didn't want to get out of the car, never mind asking for directions. We did a loop and tried to merge onto our road to Rouen.

There is a certain amount of trust involved in a marriage when navigating and driving as a team. Luckily, we have that trust. I got us out of Paris and headed in the right direction and felt a job well done. Boomie kept to the right of the road and was soon driving like a native.

Our first stop was our Airbnb in Rouen. It was a lovely house with cats and pot plants. The bed was wonderfully comfortable and the quilt one of those fluffy things that just sort of hover over you while you sleep. We just died after being on a plane for about a day and a half and then driving. It was all so typically French and a great introduction to Airbnb. I love it when a plan comes together.

We headed out west towards St Malo in Brittany. St Malo is on the coast and is a tourist magnet for foreigners and French alike. Getting there on the motorways was a dream drive. The motorways of France are fast, well maintained and everyone knows how to behave, albeit at 130km/h. Anyone who doesn't stay in the right-hand lane, except for overtaking is given a short lesson in French road rage. Everyone can lip read swear words at 135km/h and hand signals with one finger are practically universal. The motorway may have two or more lanes, but these are fast, faster and fastest. Everyone knows to keep right. It is a system that works, as long as you know what you're doing.

I had researched French toll roads and knew you could pay with a card. The toll was remarkably cheap considering the distance we could cover at warp speed. The map I was using showed when a toll could be expected. I was on countdown, my card at the ready and I had prepped Boomie on how to pay. We were so ready for our first toll. We picked a gate and I had my card ready, and it didn't work. The traffic was queuing up behind us. Nothing like irate French drivers to get you motivated. Boomie tried again and nothing. Although there are signs to say 'do not get out of your car' I jumped out and came around to the pay machine. Then a voice came over the intercom…in French of course,

I didn't get all of it, but I got enough to know I was in trouble.

And all the while the traffic queue behind us grew. These things are supposed to be quick and seamless. We were an Australian spanner in the works.

I politely said,

'We tried and cannot pay'. I gave a little shrug to the people watching me from their cars and giggled. I can't help it, but in times of stress, I giggle.

Someone started tooting at the back. I put my card up to the CCTV camera and smiled. I must have looked like an idiot.

'Wrong card,' the voice said.

I couldn't quite hear over the tooting and put my ear to the speaker.

'Wrong card.' I couldn't be certain, but I thought she said '*merde.*' (shit).

'Get in,' Boomie said. By now the queue had backed up and drivers were trying to get out of the mess. This created a rhumba dance of people backing up, three point turns and others moving to different gates all accompanied by much tooting and hand waving. I whipped out my map and hid.

We needed a Visa not Mastercard to pay. I rummaged around in my handbag and produced a card and *hey presto* the light went green and we were through.

Thank goodness the motorways in Brittany are toll free, bonus.

Way back in history the King of France negotiated with some-one in high places in Brittany to have toll free roads when the horse was the family transport. To this day the tolls are absent. This makes driving a breeze. Just another thing to like about Brittany.

Our next Airbnb was in St Lunaire just outside St Malo. We found the house while taking directions on the phone and eventually saw our man waving from his driveway. We were welcomed by a young couple and made firm friends instantly. Sometimes you just click, and they went all out to show us the hospitality of Brittany.

Wayne and Melanie had two crazy cats, Rocky and Samba. These pampered pets were spoilt and took a particular interest in Boomie and played endless scatterbrain games with him and a piece of string. They followed him around the house waiting for the next pounce. After a coffee and we'd done a load of washing, an evening was proposed at a local restaurant. We left the cats lolling around on the heater and that evening was our first experience of Bretagne galettes. Wayne and Melanie interpreted the menu to the delight of the waiter. Galettes are huge buckwheat crepes, paper thin and you choose what goes on/in them. I had ham and cheese, Boomie had a mixture of meats and then he had a dessert galette with ice-cream and berries. They are cooked on a flat pan and folded over the filling. They were washed down with a local cider. If this was French hospitality and food, I'm in.

Later we were shown around the small seaside town of St Lunaire and when we said,

'We are here to buy a house,' the first thing Wayne and Melanie said was,

'So, you like the rain?' It was a question we would hear many times on our trip.

Wayne and Melanie offered to help with our house hunting and introduced us to *leboncoin*. This is the internet market place for anything a

Frenchman has to sell and anything a Frenchman wants to buy. From a hairdryer to a house it is on *Leboncoin.* I gave Melanie our parameters and she came up with a house to see. One phone call and we had an appointment the next day.

With a promise to see our new friends and Rocky and Samba again; the next day we set off to see our first house and meet our first real estate agent.

6

Gut instinct is as good as careful consideration.

Agents have a reputation akin to used car salesmen – rats with a gold tooth. We counted ourselves savvy enough to know when we were being had. The Ashwin's weren't born yesterday. (Hire car and McDonalds just a learning curve).

The other learning curve was the weather. We didn't realise it would be so darn cold. I had looked up the average temperatures for March and we packed all we had in the way of woollies. Tropical woollies just don't cut the mustard in March in Brittany I had the foresight to pack a scarf and gloves that I'd found in a second-hand shop in Port Douglas. What they were doing there is anyone's guess. We needed reinforcements. We found the heater in the car and I put on everything I had in the suitcase. As soon as we could find a shop we'd get serious about keeping warm.

Melanie's house was situated in a small, quiet village and had the road signs screwed into its front wall. We met the son, his mother had died, and with his small son in tow were shown the house. The little boy had been brought along for English translation. He was learning English at school and was proud of his 'the cat sat on the mat' vocabulary. He was one up on us, as we could only say please and thank you.

The house was old and in the middle of a terrace of four. It had an enormous fire place and overhead oak beams in the main front room, but all the other rooms were tiny. And just to make them smaller, they were wallpapered floor to ceiling in vivid patterns and then the parents probably thought,

'Ah, what the heck. Let's do the ceiling too.' It was just a little overpowering. We were led outside and followed down a lane to the back of the house.

There didn't seem to be a backyard and in fact the whole of the back of the house was devoid of doors and windows. They had been bricked up long ago. I wondered if there was a window tax in years gone by, as in England. The house attached to the back had a date on the lintel of 1445. As our first introduction to '*old*' this was a doozy.

We thanked the son and his son and said we would ring.

'Very pleased to meet you.' The little boy said and held out his hand.

'Very pleased to meet you too.' We parted with smiles.

The first agent, in thinking ahead had drawn up a list of possibles including the house we had indicated in our first email. This again would become a familiar theme. An Ipad is a vital tool in taking videos, photos, notes etc. It would be impossible to remember all the details.

Day one and we saw 5 houses. All those hours

flat on our backs in the heat of Port Douglas trawling the internet had sharpened our skills looking at potential versus hard work and money. A house might be over 200 years old with the original oak staircase and a fireplace that could accommodate a three-piece suite, but when everything is so small, ie doorways, windows, etc how the heck to you get a bed upstairs, or a table through the front door. I was looking at things from a woman's point of view. Boomie wanted to know where the back door was. Didn't have one apparently.

The people of Brittany were, and some still are, tiny hobbit like people. They average around the 4-foot mark. We saw houses that were made for such people. The kitchen sinks in one farm house was around my thigh height. One house had a lintel that might have weighed a ton and made from the local grey granite, but it was only four and a half foot high. I saw some quaint wooden clogs in a shop window display regaling the looker with a bit of history and the clogs were teeny tiny. We told the agent we were looking for something with a bit more head room.

The other thing Brittany excelled in was flies. Being Australian, we were brought up with flies. March flies that bite through your trousers. Bush flies that stick to your back by the hundreds. House flies that are quick witted. Blow flies that are big, fat and shiny blue and lay about a gazillion eggs the minute you swat them and tiny flies that get right up your nose when riding a bicycle. In Brittany they have one variety, but considering their size they only need one variety. These black/blue suckers seek shelter and warmth in the colder months and any vacant house is a prime target. They squeeze their way inside and hang about on window sills and the floor. Not dead, but dormant. Quite a few of the houses we visited had crunchy flies underfoot. At one point I thought I had trodden on broken glass as their little crunchy bodies were squashed. We could tell right away the number of months, years the house had been vacant by the number of dead bodies. Considering none of the houses had screens we wondered on the summer months.

'Raisin toast anyone?'
'We don't have any.'
'Oh, but I thought...'

On one of our travels from A to B we stopped for lunch and found a local market. I like poking around in these village markets. What I found was a woman selling second hand clothes. I rummaged about and found a hand knitted Aran jumper. I'm a knitter and can tell when something is worth a second look. The woman selling was a canny salesperson. I asked,

'*combien?*' (how much)
'*neuf*' (nine)
It was a bargain too good to pass up. I handed over a 20 Euro note and received 5 Euro change. It wasn't what I was expecting and I must have looked a little peeved.
'*tax.*'
I wasn't happy with being duped and wanted to make a point, but Boomie nudged me. It was still a bargain and I needed something warm.
'Everyone's a winner,' Boomie said.

As I put the jumper on over my other jumper I was inclined to agree. Now all we needed was hat, scarf and gloves for Boomie.

Staying in Airbnb is a bit of a lottery. So far, we had come up winners. Our next bed was in a small village, too small to actually be on the map. We needed to telephone Horst three times to find his house.

He was renovating and the place was only half cooked. Some of the old features were still in evidence including a magnificent fire place with crackling logs giving off heat to warm us as we sat around relaxing. Horst was a school teacher and spoke enough English to make our evening instructive and fun. His bathroom wasn't so much fun. There is a peculiarity to the Breton bath. We had seen them before, but here was one in the flesh, so to speak. The bath was just over a metre and a half deep and only long enough to sit in if you don't have any legs. They also have a shelf at one end, presumably so you can get out. This bathroom was as cold as charity. Horst had rigged up a shower attachment, but to get in the bath required a quick intake of breath as the side of the cold tub hits the spot. Boomie had longer legs, but you can see the problem, or not, as the cold takes its toll on all extremities.

We shivered our way to warmth, only to step out onto freezing concrete. Horst must be made of sterner stuff. We decided that if we saw a Breton bath in a house we liked, we'd rip it out before it had a chance to complain.

As our journey progressed we became extra

critical about houses and snap decisions were getting snappier. One agent just handed over a bunch of keys and directions. Either he was very trusting, or the houses were so bad he was embarrassed. We went in search of the answer.

Nothing can compare with the house set into a rise at the back door. It was circa 1900 and a big square flat fronted monolith. Once inside it was a disaster. There had been renovations, but what struck us was the rising damp. The whole floor was sodden and splashed as we stood in the doorway. The, once white, walls were black with mould and the featured wooden framework and timber ceiling trusses were actually growing mushrooms. No wonder the agent didn't want to come with us. He probably left his rubber boots at home that day.

As we drove around the countryside we became accustomed to the left-hand drive. I would always caution Boomie that I needed to be in the gutter. This kept us on the straight and narrow most of the time. We came unstuck spectacularly in a car park after visiting Mont St Michel. This wondrous sight can be seen from the mainland, and can be reached by walking across a causeway. It is a fortified abbey on a pimple of a rock surrounded by sea started in the 8th century to become a Benedictine monastery. I had visited once before when I was a mere slip of a girl cycling around France. Nothing had changed in nearly 40 years, or in fact since the 12th century.

We parked and walked the 2km to the island and acted like tourists. It was just the thing to whet our appetite for buying a house in France. The cold wind bit into my bones, but once we arrived on the island the steep climb to the cathedral and the large steep steps were just the thing to get my blood pumping. What was once a pilgrim's walk was now an avenue of restaurants and all manner of tourist nik-naks. Tourists like eating. French tourists like eating quite a bit. They think nothing of going somewhere and then spending a goodish portion of their time indoors eating and drinking. The Ashwins are BYO sort of people. We found a sunny spot to consume our sandwiches, then did the tour, tagging along with an English group to get all the history. Boomie had to remind me that we only had one suitcase, because I'm a sucker for a memento or two and Mont St Michel has tourist mementos to satisfy even the fussiest traveller.

The French corral the visitors to this site quite well with oodles of car parks and walk ways. It was on our way out of the car park we fell into old habits and with no gutter to guide us we ended up facing the wrong side of the road. There was nowhere to do a three-point turn and as we flustered and floundered the cars began to bank up. A queue of cars is bound to get the stress levels up. I giggled, and held up our map, then tried to look like I was studying it; a ruse to not look the French in the eye. Boomie took charge and smiled then we reversed all the way out of the car park and down the road. We thought we were out of trouble when the windscreen wipers suddenly came on. You know how it is in a new car. The blinkers and wipers are sometimes opposite to what you're used to using.

'I didn't touch them.' Boomie looked around for a button or something to turn them off. I grabbed the handbook and found the word,

'*Automatique.*' Ah, another new-fangled idea that had us going for a minute. The lights we found were *automatique* too. These car manufacturers think of everything.

After our side excursion we hit the house hunting trail once more.

The real estate woman said she had several on the list, but they needed a little bit of work.

'Is this what you had in mind?' We didn't mind doing a 'bit', but when she showed us a house without stairs, and no garden, yard or fence, just a paddock, we thought we'd need to revise 'a bit' to mean a lot. How the heck were we supposed to see upstairs? Boomie would need a tractor, not a line trimmer. I fleetingly thought of sheep, but it was just a fleeting thought as Boomie jabbed me in the ribs. Things were getting a little crazy.

A few days later another agent showed us the smallest house we had ever seen. It was just 3 rooms, one on top of another with some of the floor space taken up by a staircase. It was beautifully fitted out because a Swedish family had owned it. Very modern, clean and neat, but only one person could get into the kitchen at a time. Our boat had more space.

To keep track of the houses we gave them nicknames. The Swedish house was cheap, clean and came with all the white goods. That was an advantage. Next, we saw the hat house. This was one of our short listers. The agent was an English girl and that was a big plus. The hat house was originally a hat shop in the small village. It had 2 barns, one converted to a garage and polished wooden floors with a 'rustic' kitchen including a wood fire range. It looked just right on the internet. I should point out that many houses in Brittany have roof space. They have often been converted into living areas. Some have permission attached to the property to be converted into living areas and the rest are 'just dreamin''. We often had to climb a ladder and poke our heads into the roof space to see the 'potential'. The hat house had a big loft area that might be converted by someone, but it wouldn't be us. There was quite a big hole in the roof and the rain had done its damage to the ceiling. All is not what it seems on the internet. It was a bit of a let-down to find our shortlisted house was now off the list. Of course, we could get it fixed. We could throw money at the problem. We had done that with the boat. The problem was it rankled a little that we were deceived. The agent had said it was a 'sound' property. 'Sounds alright to me!'

Then we were shown a little house in a beautiful old village square. The blue door house was quaint. It was extremely small, but so cute. It was old, but looked out onto a 13th Century church. It had a garage, but it was about a 3-minute walk away. The spiral oak staircase was original, about 200 years old, the agent said. Boomie put his eyeballs back in and I picked my jaw up from the floor. The beams in the house were one tree trunk each. We could seriously fall in love with a cute 200-year-old house, but it was just a bit too small. Perhaps in another life.

The last on the agents list was someone else's dream home. It had been in the family for years. Very comfortable, very modern kitchen with a huge stove – I'm liking it already. I could imagine cooking French cuisine on that stove.

'A bit out of our price range,' he said.

'We could save a bit more,' I said thinking of truffle soufflé.

We kept looking.

It was after this last house that we went in search of free WiFi in Josselin to keep tabs on family and friends back in Australia. We received an email to say there was a cyclone brewing in the Coral Sea and everyone was required to evacuate the Marina. Just what we needed when we were half way around the world. Our boat was sitting comfortably on the dock when we left it, now we needed to rely on other people to move it.

In situations like this there isn't much you can do except worry, bite your fingernails, keep an eye on the weather and open another bottle of red. What could we do? We advised our friends to move our boat and they kindly organised everything. We watched the cyclone every day, but it was all so far away from house hunting it didn't seem real. The cyclone passed by Port Douglas and everyone breathed easy. We put another bottle of red on the list for thankyou presents for our friends and turned our minds once again to houses.

'Now this is what I had in mind.' We were picnicking in the car park next to a river.

I pointed to the chateau owned by the de Rohan family since the end of the 15th century. It's an imposing chateau on the banks of the River Oust in the town of Josselin, with round towers and solid foundations.

'In your dreams.' Boomie cracked open a bottle of cider and I scrubbed a chateau off our list.

The photos mounted up and we began to cull the ridiculous ones and try to whittle our choice down as our appointments were coming to an end.

It was a cold morning when one of the agents said he would direct us to the next houses on the list. He hopped into the front passenger seat and asked,

'May I use your GPS?'

'We don't have one,' Boomie and I chorused. Then to our utter amazement he pressed some buttons on this big console on the dashboard and up pops the GPS. We thought it was a radio. It was in French, but that didn't matter as it was a new experience. We had a GPS on the boat, but it didn't speak to you in soothing tones. Who knew these modern fangled things were so good. We had been roaming around the French countryside with our paper map and here we had a GPS all the time.

He didn't show us any houses of note, but he did show us how to use the GPS.

Every evening in our Airbnb we'd go through what we had seen and what we liked. What we liked quite a lot were the people who share their houses on Airbnb.

Kathy lived on the Nante-Breast Canal in an old stone house. What made it special was the history. Her house was right next to a bridge over the canal. A strategic bridge in the Second World War. So, the

Germans blew it up. The shock wave went right through her house and now if you walk around the back you can see a huge crack from the foundations to the roof. We had a few days there using it as our base and became friends. The Nante-Breast Canal is a marvel of engineering. In Napoleon's time a canal was conceived to carry freight and stop the threat from the British fleet off the Atlantic coast. Work began in 1811 and then stalled until 1822, then in 1858 Napoleon III declared it open. Our guide book provided us with enough details to bring the landscape to life. We went for an evening walk along the canal tow path and relived its glory days.

That evening Kathy invited us to dinner. She had made a *Boeuf Bourguignon* and we supplied the wine. In the warm of her kitchen and enough wine, everyone speaks the same language. We had a hoot and found the French have a very good sense of humour. A lot of things are funny when you can count 4 dead bottles on the table between three people. Her husband was a woodcutter. It sounded like something out of Red Riding Hood. His job took him all over the countryside, cutting plantation forests. A bit more sophisticated than a man and an axe. He was patched in with Skype and then there were 4 people at the table and a good night was had by all.

When you are a bit maggoty from the night before and an agent says,

'Follow me,' it sounds easy enough, except he knows where he is going. We had to step on the gas to keep him in our sights. He took us all over the countryside and then we ended up in a small village looking at an overgrown little house.

He explained in stilted English,

'The old woman, she died 2 years. The family not interested.' He pushed the gate open against the crowding weeds and we trooped up the stairs to the front door and he forced it open. What we saw was a time capsule. The old lady may have died two years ago, but only the body was taken away. There was an unmade bed with her nighty still on it. A pot on the stove. The kitchen table was covered with a tablecloth and cutlery and the whole house had just ticked and creaked along for 2 years.

'It is sold with all the furniture.'

'Everything? *Tout?*'

'*Tout. Oui.*'

There was a grandfather clock. There were white goods. There were beds, table and chairs. There wasn't a key to downstairs. We peered in through a broken window and were told the boiler was only 2 years old. The yard was a mess, but it was 800 square metres. It was so overgrown you couldn't see the wood for the trees – plum trees. It was called the dead lady's house and we labelled it 'a bit of a roughie'.

We left our absolute favourite until last. This was the hill house. The thing that endeared the hill house to our hearts was that it was right next to a waterway that was navigable to big boats – you can see where this is leading.

Port Launay is a small village strung along the Aulne River and over the millenniums the river has carved out a steep valley. The banks are dotted with picturesque houses. The hill house was one of these.

The Aulne River runs through Chateaulin a large town that in days gone by relied on the river for its livelihood. The story goes that the Duke's park which is surrounded by a high wall 30km long was built in a single night by the devil in return for the Duke's soul. We were hoping we didn't need to bargain with the devil to get the house we wanted. Chateaulin with arched bridges, large stone buildings lapping the water would be extremely picturesque in summer. In March it was cold, wet and everything was covered in green moss and mould. Port Launay, just 1.2km from Chateaulin along the river was altogether more inviting. The internet pictures were taken in summer and with a glut of wildflowers surrounding it, the sparkling water and the amazing Romanesque viaduct within spitting distance it looked perfect. We waited in the morning sunshine, albeit very chilly sunshine for the agents. The British agents waxed lyrical about location, location, location. After a quick intro to the house they let us wander around and that's when the rot set in.

The house was built *into* the hill and the water run off had created a huge problem which the previous owners had neglected to address. The whole back of the house was sodden. Add to that the existence of the village spring right next to the bedroom wall and you have damp of major proportions. It might be a quaint talking point.

'Oo, and here is our very own spring,' but it doesn't do anything for the foundations of the house. It felt like a fraud. We had been pinning our hopes and dreams on the hill house. The agent pointed out the huge back yard.

'But it's practically vertical,' I said looking up the hill to a bramble of blackberry bushes while getting a crick in my neck. I had to climb like a mountain goat to get to the small garden shed and the clothes line. Who needs a carabiner to hang out the washing?

'We will let you know.' I said this with the knowledge in my own mind of sending an email as soon as we were back in our Airbnb.

We went for coffee and a big think.

Oo, look. Our very own spring!

7

Step back and breathe.

With all our appointments concluded it was time to have a bit of tourist fun. Not that we weren't enjoying passing judgement on people's houses, their tastes in furniture, their shocking decisions on wallpaper and light fittings, not to mention their bathroom arrangements.

If you have ever been to the continent you will be familiar with a squatter. This thing – loosely described as a toilet, is a porcelain tray set into the floor – or not – and has a foot pedestal both sides and a drain in the centre to aim for when doing the deed. I now know why the peasants revolted. They wanted a decent plumbing arrangement. It might be 'natural' to squat on your haunches and go for gold, but not practical. In public toilets there are no hooks to be seen for handbags, coats etc. so you need to hold everything out of the way while trying not to splash your shoes. It's tricky at the best of times. The French must have better knees than the rest of us, because I know, once I get down, it's not easy to get up again.

The flushing mechanism is archaic. It's designed to make you leave in a hurry as it spurts from a small disk in the tray and covers 4 walls, your jeans, your shoes and anything else it can reach. The chain/cistern affair is usually so black with human habitation just looking at it makes you shudder. Public or private, squatters are not for the faint hearted. If we saw a house with a squatter it was off the list. Going through the rigors of re-plumbing a house was not on our list of 'must do before I die'. In fact, one of our criteria was having the house attached to the mains drains. Septic tanks or *fosses* were out.

The tourist part of our trip was going south to visit some new friends who lived on a barge at Buzet sur Baise. Jackie and Noel were like-minded people full of derring-do and adventure.

Going south we hit the motorways and went from small hobbit houses to a definite Mediterranean flavour house. Slate was left behind as terracotta tiles took their place on the roof and we saw the occasional swimming pool in the back yard. The area is full of wineries and grapes drape themselves all over the hillsides.

Our Airbnb was a modern house overlooking vineyards and a pool. All very swish. We met the owner, Sebastian (think swarthy, handsome, young and perfect teeth and he worked in a winery!) and were shown our room and then he said he was going out. We made this Airbnb our base for visiting the area around the River Baise south of Bordeaux.

Our first stop was Jackie and Noel and lunch. The French love lunch. It stretches for 2 hours and is taken with great gusto. We went to a small village restaurant where the locals go, always a good sign.

There was a choice of three main dishes and a salad bar, then dessert. It was plain, home cooked food and delicious. But it was the conversation which will be remembered.

As Boomie and I travelled around we couldn't pronounce all the various places and so made up names that looked like they might have an English equivalent. For example, Carhaix Plouguer became Car hire plowger, St Brieuc was St Brick and the like. This was a code which we understood when talking about things.

Well it turned out Noel did the same and as he was explaining about a place close by he called it Castle Joker. We knew he meant *Casteljaloux*.

The table erupted in laughter and we knew we had made firm friends. We lingered over our lunch, so much so that I had to rouse the cook for dessert, for even the cook needs to eat her two-hour lunch. And what could be better than a stroll along the banks of the canal, where Jackie and Noel had their canal boat moored, after a sumptuous meal. It was a perfect afternoon in warm (ish) March sunshine.

Our Airbnb was quite close to the winery where Sebastian worked. We visited the shop attached to the business end of the winery and bought something to remind us of the holiday and some presents for friends. Every evening we expected our host to arrive, but Sebastian didn't come home for three days. When he finally returned I said,

'You are very trusting.'

'You look ok,' he replied.

He then asked us about our trips and I mentioned we went to Buzet sur Baise. His eyebrows raised and he asked was I sure?

'*Oui.*'

'Be very careful how you say it.' Sebastian smiled. Apparently, my pronunciation needs a little work and I'd been saying we went to fuck on Buzet. Who knew!

There was just one or two major tourist stops on our way back to Brittany and home. I had always wanted to visit the Lascaux caves. For those not in the know, there is an area in south west France in the Dordogne valley. The entire Périgord region contains one of the densest concentrations of prehistoric sites anywhere in the world. The Lascaux cave is a major attraction. You can't go in the actual cave because human fug has precipitated a fungus, but the French have made an exact replica, Lascaux II. There are other caves with original paintings and we stopped to see one of these, but naturally it was their two-hour lunch. We were on a schedule and carried on to Lascaux.

The replica was painstakingly made as an exact copy. Every lump and bump and painting was photographed, measured, copied and it all looks fabulous. I wasn't disappointed. The English-speaking guide took us through all the pictures and the theory behind them. Ticking something off one's ubiquitous bucket list is a grand feeling. I ticked one off and put another on the list. Just another reason to live in France. There is always something to see. Of course, there are things to see in Australia too. The Big Banana, the dog on the tuckerbox, Uluru, but Boomie and I were looking for new adventures in old places. We'd always been history buffs and Europe was full of it. We'd often talk about where we'd like to go. Berlin, Moscow, Paris. The list was endless. He wanted to drink a beer in the Casino at Monte Carlo and walk the WWI battlefields. I wanted to see Lake Como and Château de Fontainbleau including the apartments of Napolèon I. We'd love to house swap for Venice. It was all possible.

Heading back to Brittany we also stopped off at La Rochelle north of Bordeaux in the district of Poitou. This place has been a port since the 11th Century and in 1628 Cardinal Richelieu laid siege and 23,000 people starved to death. There was fat chance of us starving to death with more patisserie shops per square metre than I had ever seen.

We read the history in our guide book and marvelled at the biggest yachting centre on France's Atlantic coast. This is where they manufacture Beneteau yachts and we had seen them completely shrink wrapped on large trucks, perhaps heading off to new owners. The old harbour had history oozing out of its bricks and the Ashwins walked around and lapped it up.

Our Airbnb in La Rochelle was a bit of an experience. We had booked on the fly and had the merest of directions. The GPS said we were sleeping under the flight path of the local airport. Handy if you want to catch a plane, but we were looking for an apartment in the modern part of town. The streets were narrow and it all became a bit surreal when we saw a small brass band playing on a corner and passed them three times before we finally found someone and asked where the hell we were. They pointed us in the right direction and eventually we were knocking on our billet for the night.

The fellow who answered didn't speak a word of English. It sometimes happens that some people just don't have a clue what you are talking about when your pronunciation is a bit off. Hand signals, Marcel Marceau mime is no help and they can't second guess if their life depended upon it. This was Michael. He had no idea what we were trying to say and so we gave up. The room he showed us was one of two rooms in his apartment. We wondered where he would sleep, but because Sebastian had left us alone, this might be the same scenario with Michael. Our bed had one blanket and no pillows and was the bottom of a bunk. Squishy! The whole thing was surrounded by a bordello type red fringe. Kinky! And Michael had his whole wardrobe hanging on the door knob. Tricky! We settled down after eating our sandwiches then Michael invited us to sit with him. In normal circumstances that wouldn't be a problem. The only problem we could see was that we couldn't speak to one another. We all sat down on his small settee and watched a French game show. We are not show aficionados even in English and watching a foreign language could put a person off for life. With a polite yawn we excused ourselves and crashed for the night.

It was about 6am when I needed that all important bladder call and I crept out of the bordello only to see Michael asleep on the kitchen floor. He obviously needed the money our stay would provide. What a man to give up his bed. We left early, saying we didn't need breakfast, and gave him a good review on the Airbnb site.

There is an island that's connected to La Rochelle on the mainland by a long bridge. We decided to visit the Atlantic Ocean, just because we can.

Ille de Ré is thin and juts into the ocean ending with a lighthouse. The Bretons have a regional pride about their lighthouses. They are in evidence on post cards, as toothbrush holders, as tea towel pictures and just about anything you can think of that might catch the tourist eye. This particular morning the tide had receded a long way revealing ancient fish traps. It brought the natives out with rubber boots and buckets to collect mussels and anything in a shell that looked edible. They braved the cold wind to get something for free. Boomie put his hand in the Atlantic, just to say he'd done it and we retreated to our flask of coffee and cakes.

'This is what it could be like a lot of the time,' I said in the warm car with a belly full of patisserie and hot coffee.

'Hmmmm.' Boomie looked over the ocean and surveyed his future.

Our last Airbnb was with Wayne and Melanie again. They had taken us to their hearts and we stayed as friends sharing a last meal and a day out in Dinan, a medieval town with ramparts.

Dinan just fired our imagination on what we could do in France. It was your typical medieval town with cobbled streets, wood framed houses and built overlooking the Rance River. It was fantastic. There is a Gothic bridge over the river and from the ramparts we could see the valley below. We wandered the streets taking photos and drinking in the atmosphere. It made me yearn for more of France. I knew I would miss it when we left.

Our last evening was a heady experience. It turned out that the tide had receded for mussel gathering because it would be the lowest/highest tide of the year. The French go a little crazy at the lunar event. Wayne said we needed to go crazy as well, so we hopped in his car and headed to St Malo.

St Malo was once a fortified island and stands at the mouth of the Rance River. In 1944 it was heavily bombed, but the French have done a grand job at restoration. It was now a tourist mecca for high tide shenanigans. Everyone parks where ever they can find a spot. Wayne shoe horned his Peugeot onto the footpath and we tumbled out to see the crashing waves with about another 5,000 people. The French squealed and surged as the water rose to the top of the tide and the waves came over the balustrading. Then it was into the car and we whizzed around to another part of the coast to see the sea rushing through the headlands and giving a display like a blow hole. The crowds were enthralled. Boomie and I couldn't take our eyes off the traffic. The French are pushers and shovers in a crisis. The cars were parked everywhere and as people left, the crush looked like organised chaos. There was a lot of shouting, hand waving, shrugging and some choice swear words. (our French was coming along in leaps and bounds!) Somehow it all worked, as these things usually do and we came back to the house for a magnificent meal cooked by Wayne. There was smoked salmon spaghetti made with lashings of cream and then when we had made gluttons of ourselves, he brought out his father's home-made cognac. This drink was to die for. It was smooth, warming and very strong. Who can stop at one?

It was Wayne, after a few cognacs, who schooled us in what it means to be French. They take their freedoms seriously. He had a passion about fraternité, liberté and egalité. Those words meant something to him. Going to live somewhere that values freedom felt right to us. They may have idiot proof cars, but you are trusted by the Government to do the right thing. I wanted to live somewhere where you don't need to wear a bicycle helmet. Where there isn't a culture of signs or lollypop traffic controllers because someone is mowing the grass 300 metres away. In the France we had seen, the government trusted you to be an adult, to use your common sense, where people say *bonjour* when you walk past them in the street, and civilization is a 2 hour lunch.

As our time was coming to an end we had clocked up just a little over 4,000 km in our hire car, only tried to get into a different Clio once, made friends, eaten our own weight in French pastries and marvelled at the generosity, the friendly nature and the welcoming attitude of the French. If this was typical hospitality, then we would love to come and live in rural France. All we needed was a house and the good graces of the French consulate in Sydney, the department of immigration in France, the co-operation of the banks, health insurance, police checks, and enough money to throw it about the place like we didn't care. Piece of cake.

There was just one more obstacle in the way. Getting to Charles de Gaul airport to deliver our hire car.

We were coming at the ring road from the west this time and so had to travel right around half of Paris to get to the airport. We decided to try and hit the traffic around 11am. I readied for battle and punched in CDG on the GPS. We would trust to the woman with dulcet tones to get us there and I'd use the paper map as back up.

Paris is made for cars. It's a wonder people walk at all. The car is king. With our GPS we negotiated all the turn-offs and it was only when we finally reached the car park and the spiral ramp that we came unstuck. No matter what we tried we couldn't get off. Three or four times we went up and down and then I spied a broken sign propped up on the wall telling us to head off to return hire car.

We cleared out all the lollie wrappers and said goodbye to our faithful Clio.

With just one bomb scare in the departure lounge and our bags checked in we steeled our nerves and our bottoms for the long-haul flight to Australia. Decision time would come once we were on the boat and not swayed by the romance of France, the pastries, the wine, the people, the euphoric holiday mood.

We knew what we could afford. We knew what we wanted in a house. We knew we wanted to live in France.

8

Rational thought can be painful

With the last vestiges of France scrubbed from our shoes we marvelled at our 17 day, 4000km trip. All the houses crowded our thoughts and the hard decisions of *if* we would buy, what to choose, became our number one topic of conversation.

The easiest thing in the world to say to Boomie was,

'Well, what did you like?'

'You first,' he'd reply.

We took another look at the pictures on the Ipad. Each house had a memory attached. It's easy to reminisce and get a little sentimental.

'Let's be sensible,' I said. 'We have a criteria so we'll pick on the one that ticks all the boxes.'

Another solution would be to start searching again if nothing matched our needs. Our needs were:

a) mains drains – no compromise on that one.

b) A garage. This was necessary because on street parking is the pits in winter.

c) not falling down and needing *too much* work, aka, money.

d) not *too much* garden. We were envisaging travelling and seeing things, not spending our time weeding, trimming hedges and watching the grass grow.

With these absolutes set down we began the cull. The trick in all this is not to talk yourself into something. You know how it is. You see something and before you know it you have conveniently forgotten the gaping hole in the roof – just a weekend job. You neglect to take into account the rising damp – it's never been absolutely proven mould is bad for your health. And you fudge the budget to fit the desire…what's another thousand Euros. Chicken feed in the scheme of things. I'm sure we've all been there. Boomie and I tried to avoid going there. We didn't even want to look at the brochures on going there.

'Let's be ruthless,' I said.

So over a week as our French feeling left us and we gradually returned to normal, i.e. stop reminiscing and dreaming and scenarializing about how all our neighbours will love us, how I will learn French cooking, how we will buy a motorbike and travel, we began to think on things in the clear, bright Port Douglas light of day.

What we were left with was – nothing. Nothing ticked all the boxes. Nothing made our hearts skip a beat. How could we have spent thousands on air fares, car hire, Airbnb and come away empty handed.

'Well, at least we had a holiday.' That was some consolation prize. We congratulated ourselves on being uber sensible.

'Well we did say we didn't need to buy.'

'And there are *other* places. Brittany isn't the only area in France with houses to sell.'

'And we can keep saving. That's a plus.'

All these valid points were heard over breakfast, lunch, dinner and before we went to bed.

It was about a month later around April the agents stopped emailing us, when life had reverted to hum drum and we were lying on the bed in the v-berth of the boat when Boomie, once again, hashed over the houses.

He asked, 'Do you want to live in France?'

'Yes.'

'Well then, what the heck. Let's do it.'

You don't need to ask me twice.

There was one house that on reflection had ticked most, some, one or two of our boxes. The main selling point was that it was cheap, but not nasty.

I had deleted the photos of the dead woman's house, not thinking it was just what we wanted. Now it turned out it was just what we wanted. I could remember the grandfather clock. Boomie remembered the big, under the house area. I recalled the furniture in all the rooms and a marble fireplace.

'Shall we make an offer?'

'Well let's put in something low.'

'Ridiculously low. It's been on the market for 2 years. They might be desperate.'

The French are no different than anyone else when it comes to commerce. It's spelt the same and they generally want a good deal like anyone else. We notified the agent we were interested in the dead woman's house and asked what would be the next step. The agent said – via google translate – that he would put an offer to the owners. We put a price on paper, all the while telling ourselves that we didn't need to buy it if we didn't want to.

It took a few days for a, 'No,' to come back.

Now it became a game of strategy, cat and mouse and psychology. Because we couldn't look the owner in the eye and call their bluff we had to extrapolate, second guess and use a bit of 'what if'. The Ashwins are good at all of the above. We figured they hadn't had a bite for 2 years. They didn't want the property considering they hadn't even cleaned it out after the old woman died. Our guess was that they were ready for the taking. We'd let them stew.

Of course, if they had waited 2 years they could quite probably wait 2 more. People are fickle like that. The agent emailed and said in a veiled attempt to prompt us that he thought the owners would accept another offer to the amount of… We waited and then upped our offer just a little.

'No.'

Wanna play hard ball eh? Well we didn't give two hoots whether we bought the house or not. So, go stick that in your pipe and smoke it. Negotiations can be quite fraught with emotions.

We didn't want to beg, but being denied something makes you a bit frantic. As the keeper of the finances I knew down to the last Euro/dollar what we could afford. Our last offer- the one they rejected, was it. There was no more. We emailed the agent and said just that.

'We cannot offer any more.'

They sat on the information. You can imagine the smug look on our faces as we thought on the hand wringing happening in France.

'Madame, Monsieur, it's been 2 years. Take the offer.'

'But, but.'

'Take it.'

'Oui.'

I think we just bought a house in France!

9

A Journey starts with one step. Obviously, Confucius never bought a house in France.

Now the gamble really began. We wanted to live in France, but needed permission from the consulate and a house before we could apply. If they said,

'No,' then it was all over red rover. We would have bought a house we can't live in. Surely the French could see we were serious. Surely, they couldn't deny us once we had invested. We were willing to pay their fees. It was like playing Russian roulette with our money.

The other gamble was finding a Renoir in the attic. Finding treasure (*trésor)* in the garden. Those shows on television have a lot to answer for in the way of expectations. We might have a Napoleonic horde under the house. We could well have a long-lost painting from the impressionist era just propped up behind the door. These things happen you know!

Our family actually were not surprised, or dismayed at our thoughts to go and live in France. Just another hair-brain scheme from their adventuring parents.

But before we could do anything serious, like signing anything, we found out there was more than one person that wanted our money. It turns out that the buyer pays for the advertising and agent's fees. The buyer pays for the Notaire (solicitor who deals with houses). The buyer, if they are sensible and wanting to negotiate all the French hoo-harr, engage a mortgage broker and pay them and the buyer pays for all the bank fees for a French bank account. It was a recurring theme throughout the agonising 6 months to follow.

French bureaucracy is an art form. If you thought filling out a tax return was onerous you haven't begun to scratch the surface in red tape. Did I mention we don't speak French?

Apparently, there are steps one must take in purchasing a house before A, B, or C can be completed. Luckily for us we engaged a mortgage broker who was fluent in the whys and wherefores of buying a house in and from a foreign country. Emma soon became our best friend in the whole world. She would be worth every dollar.

We had decided to go for a mortgage, because French banks were falling over themselves to lend money at ridiculously low rates. I knew we could service a debt with so little interest. Our eyes would always be on the exchange rate, but we figured sometimes you win, sometimes you lose.

Buying a house in France is a bit like operating in code. There are names (unpronounceable to an Anglophile) for each step. The first step was to secure the property as ours and stop some gazumping. Gazumping is when someone comes under your offer and bumps you out of the picture. There would be fat chance of that happening. The house had been on the market for 2 years with nary a bite.

To secure it as ours wasn't too tricky. We just had to sign a paper to say the offer was backed financially. Well, that is all very well, but it turns out that because we wanted such a small mortgage and Boomie was deemed in his declining years we were 'ineligible' to all the major lenders. They obviously wanted the high rollers. The mortgage of 100,000 Euros minimum. We had a sizable deposit so wanted what amounted to them as just an inconvenience sum. Chicken feed in the scheme of things.

Emma had to scour high and low to find a bank that would come to the party.

Meanwhile our time limit on our offer was ticking down like a clock on a game show.

Once you have the funds secured then you can submit your offer in writing and once accepted then you get a certain amount of days to look over the diagnostics reports.

I don't know why it is that when the French wanted something it must be done in a hurry. It needs to be priority and they put asterisk on everything. When we want something done in a timely manner they think nothing of taking a week, a month, sometime before the next coming, to send the papers through.

The diagnostics – which are paid for by the owner just for a change – are very official with stamps, accreditation certificates attached and other official documents to say the people doing the diagnostics have letters after their names etc. We received four reports. One for electrics, one for plumbing, then pests and construction. They were thorough, exhaustive and all in French. Google translate can only do so much, so we sought French help.

I have a market stall in Port Douglas and sell my books every Sunday. I meet all sorts of people including French tourists. I'm always on the lookout for a French accent.

First, I found Sophie. She was from Paris and I needed help with our banking. I had tried to log into our French account without success. I needed someone to ring Paris for me and be on the internet at the same time. Sophie was that person. She was backpacking around Australia and had time on her hands. We offered her a meal and wine and with a handshake we met that evening. She hopped into the dinghy and we ferried her to our boat, which we had decided to put up the inlet and save on Marina fees. We needed every dollar we could get.

'You like rain?' she asked.

There was a lot of talking, a lot of waiting with muzac, and quite a bit of –press one-for help, press two-for fed up, press three-for starting again. When we finally contacted the bank we were attended by Alex la Grande.

Alexander the Great really was great. He walked Sophie through our problems and with a small tutorial I was connected. Sophie taught us a few new swear words too. She also introduced us to the idea of a *crèmaillére*. This is a housewarming party. It is called the hanging of the pot. The home owners supply the guests with alcoholic libations and food and everyone has a good time. We thought this might be a good idea for the future and stored the word away for further discussion.

'Of course I will come,' Sophie said.

Her talents were boundless. We had the feeling we were going to really like France and the French.

Next to help was Cedric. He was from Nante and on holiday with his family. A promise was made for him to come down to the boat and just read through our diagnostics for us. As it happened Cedric had spent a couple of years in Brisbane, Queensland so his English was good.

'So, you like the rain,' he said.

We found, from Cedric's reading, we had ancient electrics, the drains were where they should be, we didn't have active pests although there was evidence and the house, at 70 years old, wasn't about to fall down. The French, if nothing else are thorough. With each diagnostic report was a list of 'to do'. There was the urgent stuff in the expert's opinion. There was the stuff that could wait, but not too long, and then there was the stuff that would need to be fixed before the nuclear holocaust. We could live with that. Cedric waved away our concerns and the work to be done.

'It is a sound house.' We gave him a bottle of red for his trouble and promised to keep in touch. Once again, the French endeared themselves to us with their willingness to help.

Julius was our last helper. He was backpacking around the world and busking. He was very good at Spanish guitar. He was also very good at reading legal documents. We passed a few his way and he gave us the lowdown on what we were signing. It was comforting to know what was in the fine print.

The forms with fine print kept filling our inbox and our PO Box. There is a history to every house. Ours was no different. We found out that the old woman who died was Bernadette Cansot and she was married to Louis Cansot. They had two daughters who inherited the house. The documents also state the ages and marital status and addresses of the daughters. They had moved away from the village, but not that far. I felt a bit like a genealogist or a spy, delving into other people's lives. They could see all our documents too, so it was a bit of a trade-off.

Napoleon, way back, when he was Emperor, had a few bright ideas. He was a smart cookie. He made a law to say the property of the family must remain in the family through inheritance. You can't just bequeath your house to the cat's home or someone who fixed your plumbing. So the two daughters had inherited the house and wanted nothing more than to get rid of it. We could oblige them.

Did I mention I love the internet. We could sign and scan all the documents and send them back via email. Just imagine trying to do it all by snail mail, impossible.

The French are very pragmatic. They accepted our signatures without a qualm. In Australia you need everything original or duly notarised. The French bank was obliging too. They processed everything, albeit in triplicate. Why does everyone want to know when you were born? I must have written my details a thousand times and we were only about 3 months into the delicate negotiations.

There is a time when the house buying comes to the 'no going back' period. This is when all the parties are in agreeance and what is set out in the contract is set in stone, because we are in accord. I wanted to make sure that what we saw on that day when we pushed the door open was still going to be there.

Call me suspicious, but it would be so easy to do a shifty on the Australians and the house furniture to be taken 'by mistake' never to be seen again.

'Oh, you mean *that* grandfather clock. That wasn't actually in the contract.'

'Um, well, we really didn't think you wanted the three-piece suite.'

I read all the fine print with a French/English dictionary to hand and found the clause which guaranteed that all was as we saw it. The very last signing of both parties is supposed to be at the house so you can verify for the last time that the doors are still there, if you bought a roof it's still on and all that sort of thing. Thinking on human nature, why would you stipulate both parties come to the party if there hadn't been some dodgy dealing in the past? People don't make these rules for the hell of it.

Anyway, because we couldn't just nip back to France our real estate agent had to be a proxy. More forms to sign, more money to spend. The Notaire needed to be present and he didn't come cheap. We all know how solicitors' charge like wounded bulls.

Our Notaire was no different. We waited with baited breath for the confirmation email. This exchange of documents meant the house offer was accepted. It meant that the party of the first part and the party of the second part were in accord and we could now proceed to give over our life savings, the daughters would duly receive them from the Notaire and everyone could sleep easy at night.

All must have happened according to plan because we received the bill.

Now Emma, our mortgage broker really went to work. She worked with the bank to get our documents in order. We needed signed copies of everything to do with the house. There were 'sign here' stickers coming at us from all directions. I just about gave up trying to decipher what was what in French. Boomie and I had our own copies to sign. We had joint copies to initial and sign and we had other documents that needed to be notarised. This is when we hit a small problem. Where do you find a JP, who speaks French, to witness a signature? The JP we approached in Mossman – population around the 4,000 mark –said she couldn't do it. She couldn't sign something she couldn't read. There was a frantic bit of ringing around to find the elusive French speaking lawyer, but with no success.

I emailed Emma and outlined the problem. She passed on the information and as pedantic as the French may be in regard to bureaucratic procedure they seem to be pragmatic. A quick shrug of the shoulders and our problem was solved. It will do! Our life didn't depend on having a notarised form. It was the French way of dealing with a problem and I liked it.

We had been paying our bills along the way to avoid a cardiac arrest at the end and that way you don't quite realise how much you are handing over. It makes the whole business of paying a little more pleasant. As the wind down began we felt we had done quite well. Most of the fees were done and dusted and we still had money in the bank, the French mortgage would kick in once things were settled and there were no surprises.

Except the Notaire sent his bill. It looked like he was charging for the air he breathed. I queried it with Emma and she said it was 'normal'. That's easy for someone else to say, not so easy for us to swallow. But what can you do? We paid.

Then we found out the French bank charged for everything. And I mean everything. The Australian banks have a reputation for blood sucking, but they are mere mosquitoes in comparison to the French Vampires.

We were charged a fee to put our money in the bank. They wanted a fee to keep it there. They decided they would take a bit to service the mortgage and then there was a charge to take money out. Plus, we had to pay for a cheque book. Who the heck has a cheque book these days? The bank also wanted – a stipulation in law- life insurance for Boomie re the mortgage. I could bump him off and the house would be paid in full. We also had to buy house insurance.

'How much?' It was that old familiar catch phrase. Lastly the bank had the audacity to open a second account for us and deposit some of our mortgage money in it and charge us for the pleasure. Whose money is it anyway?

Six months dealing with French documents, French banks and French paperwork is an education.

I may not be able to speak the language, but I know a bit about how to buy a house. It was stressful at times, but the end result was on the 22 September 2015 we finally could say without a shadow of a doubt that we had bought a house in France – after looking at it for 20 minutes, 7 months ago. We hoped we'd done the right thing. It was only when we received the final papers in the post it became real.

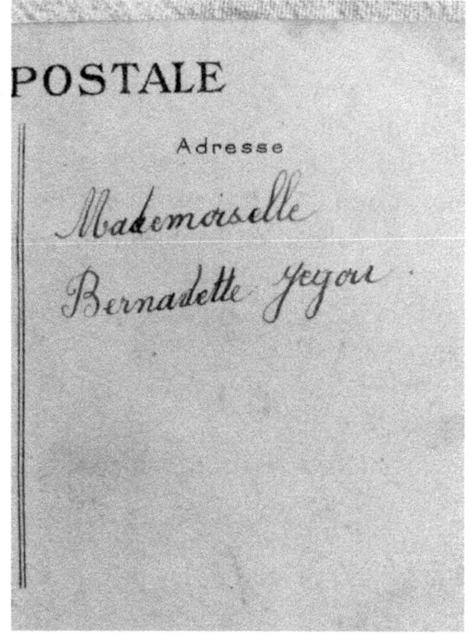

A letter to Bernadette

10

All good things come to those who wait, and wait, and wait.

I once again went to the French consulate site on the internet and ran though their list of requirements. They were extensive, exhaustive and joy, oh joy, in English.

We needed a raft of documents to take to the consulate in person. We had to submit them in the order they stipulated on their list. We needed to make an appointment for submission and get a verification date, a security number for entry and then they say,

#There will be no refunds under any circumstances.

#If you do not have all the documents required at your interview you will be rejected.

In other words, we would only get one shot at getting the first stage of a residency permit. I better get it right!

Everything needed to be timed to the day. Our police check could not be more than three months old. Ditto for our bank statements, our letter from the bank and about a dozen other documents regarding who we were, where we were going, why we were going there and how long did we intend to stay. We also needed health insurance and our airline tickets.

We coughed up for tickets to Sydney for February, and then tickets to France for May and travel insurance for a year that included health. Then I went online to the consulate web page and booked our interviews. I picked 12 midday and 12.20 for Boomie. The Consulate, being French, went for a two-hour lunch. We assumed we would be the last before lunch so we'd have a little more time if needed. The last time I went for an interview I was nervous as hell. This one, I presumed, would have me on the edge of my seat too. But if all went according to plan then we would have the first step in our passports to being able to reside in France.

I felt like I was at Houston control. I made a timeline with a big sheet of paper and kept track of what was going in, out, coming back, getting done etc. It was nerve wracking knowing we needed all the tick and flicks before we left for Sydney, because we only had one chance.

As all our documents were gathered I went over and over to make sure we had duplicates and they were in the right order as stipulated. God forbid the French had to hunt for the police check because it was *after* the health insurance. Unthinkable!

I booked an Airbnb and our travel arrangements were set. It was gamble time.

We lay on the bed in the heat of a tropical summer and thought on the likelihood of being rejected. We had complied with all the requirements. We had everything they wanted. What could go wrong? If we could weather the red tape of buying a house in Brittany, then the Sydney interview would be a cake walk. We were nice people for heaven's sake.

I love public transport. Sydney is full of it and getting around is a breeze. I had googled the office block where the Consulate took up a whole floor and knew where to go. The Ashwin's are never late. The consulate had said that we should not be early, because there are no facilities to wait. Boomie and I milled around downstairs for about 20 minutes and then made our way in the lift to the hallowed French ground. The first thing that met us was the *tricolore* flag. The small anti chamber was cut off from the consulate by a glass wall. Obviously to keep the riff raff out. We were expected and the concierge took our booking numbers and with a quick phone call pressed the buzzer and the glass doors opened. We went in like two school kids summoned to the headmaster's office.

When they said 'interview' we assumed we would be taken to a private room and over a mahogany desk our documents would be perused, our characters discussed and our hands shaken as we were accepted into the fold of French life.

What we got was a woman behind a glass teller screen. Boomie had a hard time hearing through the glass and so I had to translate.

'Where are you living?'

'Brittany.'

'So, you like the rain?'

The French have a sense of humour. Always a good start.

We proudly handed over our documents. They were rifled through, photocopied, a file made in our name and then the woman asked,

'You don't intend to work while in France.'

'No.'

'Well you need to have this declaration form filled out and witnessed.'

My heart felt like it was in my throat. Our one chance up in smoke. I couldn't breathe. I felt like crying. House, money, tickets, money…all for naught. On the application it said *either* fill this section out *or* make a stat dec. Now Madam said we needed a stat dec.

'There is a JP at the chemist downstairs. You could do it now.'

'Now?'

'Oui. We will wait. We close for the day at 12.30.'

Sweet Jesus. We had 10 minutes to race downstairs and get it signed and bring it back.

Boomie and I ran out of the office and waited for the lift. They always take ages when you are in a hurry. We ran around to the chemist only to be told they didn't have a JP and the consulate were always doing this to them. Where could we go as the minutes ticked by?

'The Town Hall have one.'

Now, I'm not bragging, but I have a very keen sense of direction. I take note of where I am and how to get there. Now I knew that the Sydney Town Hall was just 2 blocks away. We ran.

We went to the main entrance and were directed around the back. Of course, the back of the Town Hall is almost a city block away. We skitted down the steps and ran to the back door and rushed inside and found the JP. He was chatting to his last customer and I couldn't stand it, talking about chicken or something, so I butted in,

'Please we are in a hurry. We only have,' I looked at my watch,

'5 minutes.' I'm not sure, but I think I sounded like a panic-stricken maniac. I felt sick. 'We're not going to make it,' I said to Boomie.

'Ok.' The JP took our docs. He must be the slowest reader on the planet. He read mine and then started to read Boomies.

'They are identical.' I said. 'You just need to sign please.'

'Alright young lady.' The JP looked at me. Boomie kicked me under the table.

He signed and then brought out his blotter. Oh, for God's sake. I took a breath and waited and then as soon as he was done I snatched those suckers off the table and we were off. I reckon I broke the 4-minute mile back to the Consulate, with Boomie right on my heels. I looked at my watch as the lift took us at a glacial pace up the floors to the office. 12.32.

'Grrrrh'.

The doorman was there and smiled as he ate his sandwich. He let us in and we went right up to Madam and handed over our docs. She looked completely unfrazzled about the whole thing, like it happens all the time.

Now if it was me, I would have taken a look through the docs while the applicants were away having a heart attack and running through the streets of Sydney like bank robbers. But no, she now began again to go through our application.

There was one problem.

Fuck! What now.

Well it turns out that in our wisdom we had elected to start our travel insurance for the Sydney trip, sensible precaution I thought.

'No.'

We needed our insurance to start when we arrive in France in May. That way the one-year visa and the insurance will be contemporary.

'How…can…' I couldn't speak. I was devastated. All this stress and we were stymied at the last hurdle. I wanted to throw up. Boomie visibly drooped.

'Can you get the company to change the date?'

I said 'yes' although I had no idea.

'Just email us the new document when you get home. Within two days. OK.'

God, I love the French pragmatism.

'Ok,' I managed to croak. I relaxed, just a little. Boomie coughed up his tongue that he had swallowed.

'We can just email it through?'

'Oui.'

'Thank you.'

They kept our passports and all our documents. That was a good sign. They took our photographs and biometric prints. We would now be fingerprinted in the EU. We paid our fees and walked away giving ourselves a high five.

I got straight on the phone and rang our insurance. Why is it I always get the Indian trainee? He didn't have a clue what I wanted. I asked for his supervisor. She didn't have a clue either, except to say we should go back to the people who sold us the policy.

That was the first sensible suggestion they had given me. Flight centre spoke English, they were in the high street of Port Douglas and the girls knew us quite well. We would just wait until we arrived home. Anything is possible. If we could buy a house in France then changing a date on our policy was child's play.

It took a bit of swift talking back at Flight Centre, but we managed to get things sorted and duly sent off the email. Then we waited.

The stipulated 10 days passed and we waited.
'Must be the post.'
'Well, they did need to wait for the email.'
'Australia post are shocking for service.'
'We are not the only ones wanting visas. They are busy I guess.'
We waited.
'Are you sure you had all the docs?'
'Yes.'
'Sure?'
Then miracles do happen.

First Boomie's, then mine turned up in the post. And inside our passports were French visas. They allowed us multiple entries for a year. The one tricky bit was that we needed to activate our multiple entry visa within three months of issue. The instructions were clear. When we arrived in France we must photocopy the visa with the entry stamp and send all our paperwork to the OFII. (Office of Foreign immigration). The Consulate gave us the address in

Rennes. They even highlighted it so there could be no mistake.

All we needed to do now was go to France, fill in the forms, get all the documents together and apply to the OFII in our region for an interview, get a medical and the all-important Titre de sejour stamp would be put in our passports and we could call ourselves residents. Then all we needed to do was renew for the next 5 years at the prefecture in our district and Bob's your uncle, or Marcel in this case.

It all sounds so easy when you say it with a red wine in your hand and you have been through the rigors of buying a house in France.
'Pfffffffhhh. A doddle.'

11

Goods and chattels can accumulate like slut balls under the bed.

We thought we had rid ourselves of stuff. All the junk we collected had been purged from our lives. We even went as far as to tout our lifestyle as minimal. Not Japanese minimal, but utilitarian none the less. I had just enough of everything and no more. So when we decided to send some 'stuff' to the house I had the vague idea about one cubic metre. Just a few bits and pieces and some new towels, sheets etc. Nothing major.

Then I remembered my books. I had collected quite a few when we still had a house. They had been boxed and fostered – or should that be foisted – at my girlfriend's house. I had been without them for 11 years, but they were not forgotten, not by me anyway.

Lori and Peter lived in Townsville and so to get my babies back necessitated a road trip of 400 km each way. It was a small price to pay to see my treasures again.

After a wine or two, a fond farewell and the books packed in the ute, we headed north to consolidate our stuff. Our daughter came to visit and brought my trusty sewing machine. This machine was as old as me and had been from Switzerland to Australia then the UK, back to Australia and was now being shipped to France. We went shopping for some household stuff, and added to the pile in the storage shed. My one cubic metre began to grow. When did we manage to collect all this stuff? The removalist said an estimation of three months door to door. The stuff would arrive before us, and we didn't even have a front door key. Oops.!

Naturally shipping to France requires a mountain of paperwork. It wouldn't be France without it. The removalist gave us a quote and we set a date.

Psychology is a much-studied phenomenon. No sooner had the price been set than we started to try to squeeze in just a little bit more. Tools, clothes, bed linen all were added to the pile. They wouldn't notice a few more bits and bobs, would they?

The day came and our goods and chattels were boxed and gone – to France – we hoped. Four cubic metres of our collective junk. I tackled the paperwork.

We needed a form –in French – to say all our goods were household items. Not for sale. Who would want our decrepit stuff anyway? It might not be pretty or fancy, but it was paid for and it was all we had. That's about the sum of it. The French wanted an inventory in French and English with a value on everything in Euros. We tried, but when you are sending a Bunnings, (our preferred hardware store) extension cord which has been with you for 8 years through thick and thin it's hard to put a price on it. We valued it at about one Euro. Really when you look at things you have collected it's never worth much in the dollar sense, but it's priceless in the emotional attachment. I had little mementos from my travels I'd stored for years. I had a box of Valentine's Day card from the kids, priceless and worthless at the same time.

Our whole lives amounted to less than $5,000. Not much for a lifetime of experiences. Translating everything via google was a doddle. Google translate should get a medal. We gave ourselves a high five and I emailed the real estate agent regarding the likely-hood of her being available to let the removalist into the house on a particular day.

The original agent had moved on and in her place was a woman who didn't speak English. I outlined our problem via email and was met with silence. The agent still had the key to the property so on the face of it, things couldn't be easier. There was a lot of miscommunication and kerfuffle before we finally brokered a deal where the agent would make a date at their choosing for the goods to be let into the house. Time is money they say and her time was our money. Oh well, just another bill to pay. What we did find out was that it is the agent's duty to get the electricity and water connected. That was a bonus for us. She had arranged for the meter men to come the day after we arrived and connect us to the grid. That would only mean one night without utilities.

After the boxes had arrived the agent sent the only key in the post and were on countdown to our fly out date in May. This time we didn't have a hire car, but would be relying on public transport to get us home. It felt good to be saying that word and knowing it was our very own house. It still felt a bit unreal, no matter the paperwork, the angst, the running around and the photocopying we had done.

When you buy a house in a small village there isn't a lot of choice on the bus service. Once or twice a day and that's about it. I went into overdrive trying to co-ordinate the transport to arrive in daylight hours. What I didn't reckon on was that daylight hours extend, in May, to about 10:30pm.

Our travel arrangements were straightforward as long as everything went to plan.

We had to catch a bus to Cairns airport, one hour, booked in advance. A Flight from Cairns to Hong Kong then on to Paris, 27 hours in total. From there a bus to the train station Montparnasse, 1 hour 15 minutes approx., which services the west of the country. Three hours on the TGV and we would be at St Brieuc. From there an hour to our village by bus.

The last time we had been to the house we were in the agent's car. I had, of course, google mapped it and knew where we needed to hoof it to get to our street. What we never realised in all our negotiations was that it was up a hill. It just didn't occur to look at the topography of the place.

We had packed heaps of stuff in our second hand $20 suitcases from the charity shop and now their woeful wheels had to do duty up a hill. Why we brought so much I will never know. We lugged our cases, (while wearing our cranky pants), up and up. After about 30 hours travel one is bound to get a bit tetchy. My eyes were hanging out and Boomie's patience was fraying at the ends.

There was a tense moment when my navigational abilities were left wanting and then I re-booted and we were on the home stretch.

Seeing the object of our hopes and desires in the flesh again was kinda exciting. I had seen the outside so many times on google earth I knew every slate roof tile, every bush, every bit of the guttering and steps. To be standing in front of it for the first time as owners was a big thrill. Never mind the overgrown hedge, the choking letter box full of advertising. This was our house.

12

Expectations and reality rarely make good bedfellows.

As we opened the door we saw all our boxes from Australia piled up in the kitchen. They were a welcome sight. Long haul flights sap every bit of energy from you. We were running on empty and wanted nothing more than to go to bed.

There were three bedrooms to choose from and we took the one out the back, because the other two had signs of habitation and until I could reconnoitre the place I didn't want to sleep in someone else's bed…on a bed where an old woman died. A natural concern. The room we chose was dank, smelly and soon to be christened Colditz. It was like a freezer in there.

I rooted around in the boxes for some blankets and sheets and made the bed and we crashed. In the night I raided my suitcase for clothes to lay on the bed and wear as it was as cold as the hair on a polar bear's bum in that little room.

I woke up with a tongue like the bottom of a bird's cage, but with no water to the house it was a case of finding that one last barley sugar and suck.

As the morning light crept into the room we surveyed our surroundings for the first time and one thing became pretty obvious straight away. The Cansot sisters, Madame Marie and Madame Jeannine, had cherry picked the property. Everything that was supposed to be there, ie the grandfather clock, was gone. Everything that couldn't fit through the door, stayed.

'Oh, you mean *that* mahogany sideboard, settee and rocking chair.'

At least they had swept the floors of flies.

I was so looking forward to sorting through Bernadette's belongings, looking for treasures, memories and just fossicking into someone else's' life. All gone.

Boomie was pragmatic.

'Less shit to throw away'. I have a rather large sentimental bone when it comes to that sort of thing.

The first thing we needed to do was beg some water. I had come armed with a dictionary, a phrase book, a picture dictionary and of course ol' google translate. I went in search of a bucket and waited until I saw a neighbour and went out with my best French.

'*Bonjour.*' It was a good start. I pointed to our house, my bucket and made a drinking motion.

'*Eau? S'il vous plaît.*' The woman took my bucket and closed the window on me. I stood around for a bit looking stupid and then she re-appeared with water.

'*Merci.*'

We could have a coffee as long as the stove worked. Naturally I had packed some zip lock bags for the occasion. Boomie was suitably impressed

90

with my forward planning. All we needed was cups…I'm not perfect.

Toileting was another matter. The little pink and brown toilet stood sulking because there was no water. I begged another bucket from the *Carrosserie* (crash repairers) across the road. They were more than helpful, even offering us their toilet.

'*No, merci.*' With a bucket we could at least flush the toilet, but only the once. We did get about 50 toilet paper rolls. These were the very cheap variety and the French had a way of packing them into the smallest plastic bag by squashing them flat. Obviously, they don't fit on a toilet roll holder after being squished, but they were welcome.

We had been told our electrics were ancient. A helpful euphemism for cactus. The regulations in France, and you can guess there are many, state that if you buy a house and its electrics are old then you must upgrade to an RCD breaker at the very least. We didn't have one and assumed our electricity could not be connected until we were suitably protected. It is the job of the real estate agent to arrange the electrics for the new owners. We had been given an appointment first thing in the morning. Knowing a thing or two about tradesmen and French bureaucracy I didn't put my expectations at a high level. I was suitably impressed when the fresh faced young man knocked on our door promptly at 9.15, handed us a piece of paper and went to work on our connection.

I asked about the ancient fuse box and he just shrugged, read the meter then, with a smile and a handshake, locked everything with those little wire tamper proof twists and was gone. We were good to go. There was that pragmatism again. I was sure I was going to like living here. Either the French were wonderfully 'can do' people or on the other hand they didn't give a shit. Either way it impressed us.

The water fellow, arranged by the agent once again, was equally quick and efficient. If this was how things worked in France, we were rapt. The other thing that captivated me was their billing procedure. Just give them your bank details and they automatically take out a given fee once a month for major utilities. If at the end of the year they read your meter and you have paid more, then you get a refund. They then take an average and readjust your payment. Simple.

Day one and we had electricity and water, but still no coffee.

I had assumed there would be a cupboard full of plates, cups, saucers, bowls etc. We did have 4 saucepans so boiling water wasn't an issue once we managed to get the stove alight without blowing ourselves up. I say this because every time we turned on the gas we could smell a leak. The French are not too safety conscience when it comes to the house and most people keep their swap and go bottles in the kitchen next to the stove in a cupboard, for example, under the sink. I have a good nose for these things and as I poked my head under the sink it was overwhelmingly obvious our connection was leaking.

We had eaten all our barley sugars for *petit*

déjeuner (breakfast) and needed something more. We went shopping and bought 2 cups, two plates, two bowls, a microwave bowl and an electric kettle. Thinking on food we went for something simple and really when you think about it anything goes with wine. Wine is a staple in France.

As luck would have it Bernadette left an ancient microwave. It had just one dial and a very loud ping. Straight out of the '80s. I could be inventive and cook everything on ping setting until we could get someone to look at the stove.

Where do you start in an old house? The first thing we needed to do was make our bed more comfortable. There were three bedrooms each sporting a double bed. The sisters couldn't be bothered to lug the mattresses out the door. The beds were matched with carved bed heads and out of the three we found one that looked relatively new; I'm talking stains. There is just something nasty about stains on a mattress. And we just hoped Bernadette didn't take her last breath in the bed we would make our own, although there was a sizable dent where she, or someone, had slept.

One of the best things we had shipped over was the Dyson vacuum cleaner. It has a mighty powerful suck. With its attachments attached I sucked the life out of and back into the mattress. We picked the bedroom with the new windows and roll down shutters and I got to work making it homely. I defy anyone not to get a bit carried away when you are re-arranging furniture. There was a wardrobe already in the room and I could see right away it would never fit through the door, so it must stay. Getting the placement of a bed can be a trying affair. I roped in Boomie and we tried various positions, (keep your mind out of the gutter), until his back said,

'Here will do.'

Considering how cold we were when we first arrived I felt my life wouldn't be complete without a quilt. Madame Marie and Madame Jeannine had left a few sheets and blankets and one really nice (new looking) double bed quilt cover.

On the continent they do quilts really well. I have slept under quilts that are all goose down and wonderfully warm. I've had the pleasure of sleeping under 10★ thermal efficiency stars and boiled in my own juices. And I've slept under quilts that look fabulous, but have as much warmth as a cotton tea-towel. I wanted a quilt. So we went shopping. The one good thing about our village is that it has the fortune to be near a really big supermarket. It is just a 15-minute walk down the hill. *Super U* has a bit of everything and then some. They did quilts.

Getting something that suits everyone's sleeping habits is a bit of a compromise. In the end we opted for 4★ thermal efficiency. Boomie has about an 8★ star rating all his own. I went to work fussing about making the bedroom 'nice'; a girl thing.

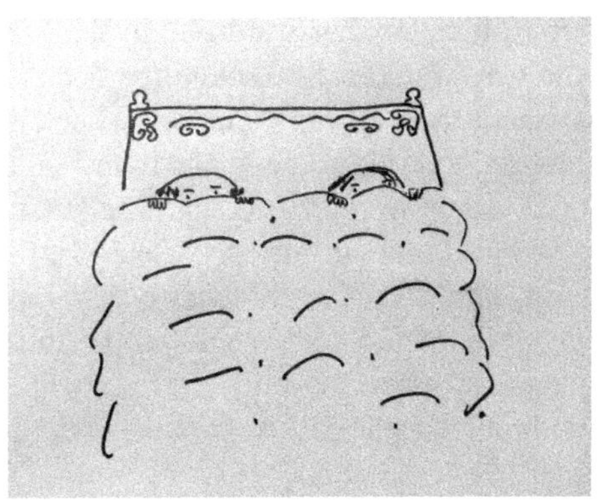

4★ *Thermal efficiency*

In Brittany they have a really, quite weird, custom when it comes to pillows. In Australia we have rectangular pillows, sometimes two. In Brittany they have the sausage. This contraption is a long pillow that both occupants share. Their pillowcases are about 2 metres long. Sort of like a sleeping bag for a snake. Bernadette had three of these pillows, and although we could sleep on a second-hand mattress without too much trouble, using someone else's pillow is out.

Super U do pillows…well sort of. They have the snake sleeping bag type and then they have a huge square pillow filled with feathers. We went with feathers. They feel great, but as for neck support, they are useless. Still, they do look nice on the bed. Homemaking is such fun.

The next job was to unpack all the boxes crowding the kitchen. This was like Christmas.

There was a nice-looking wardrobe in the lounge room…no way would it fit through the door…and so I commandeered this for a temporary book case. I had managed to bring some books in my suitcase and squeeze some in my backpack. The latter felt as heavy as lead and cut into my shoulders like a knife, but I didn't want to attract any unwarranted attentions from the flight attendants so pretended it was light as a feather and only held a credit card and a toothbrush. I think I just got away with it on the airline.

Being reunited with my babies after all this time was wonderful. Boomie and I spent a leisurely day putting our books away, reminiscing about when we bought them, who gave what to whom and had fun in the process. We also had photo albums and these were laughed over with a bottle of Cab Sav and some cheese.

Our house was becoming our home as we put things away.

Paperwork is never far away and it was fortunate that *Super U* have a photocopier. Our OFII papers were copied and we went to the post office to send them registered post.

You never can be too careful. The post office has a convoluted entry system. You go into the anti-room and press a button which alerts the woman behind the desk someone is waiting to come inside. She buzzes you in and the other door unlocks. All very serious and security conscious. We outlined what we wanted with hand signals and a smattering of French. All good apparently. I gave Boomie a high five as we exited the post office. Job done.

Back home we took a good long look at what we had bought and what the Cansot's had left us. We had 4 wardrobes, one was circa 1860 made from oak. We had three beds, two with carved bed heads. We had a toilet that should have had the design engineer at the factory sacked. It was pink with a brown seat! We had two fireplaces without a chimney. In the kitchen we had a wood stove that hadn't worked for donkey's years and was made of cast iron and a gas stove that was threatening to blow up. Things were looking good. Oh, and the fridge didn't work. Ditto for the chest freezer downstairs. And the washing machine was missing.

The light fittings were suitably French and quite hideous. The one in the kitchen was slung so low Boomie hit his head on it and it smashed to the floor. One less thing to thrown out. We had a circa 1960 monstrosity that was all cut plastic in yellow and threw fantastic shapes on the ceiling. But the *piéce de resistance* was in the front bedroom. Picture this. A light fitting made of wood which comes down on a turned column of rings and ends in four arms. On each arm is a wooden clog. A shoe! Then under the shoe is a glass light shade and the bulb. Splendiferous. *Magnifique.*

Surely the French had a bit of taste. Not by the look of it. If you remember the 1970s then you will remember the craze of taking some wood looking dye and with a rag going over a wooden door or door frame to make it look like…well…wood. We had every door and frame done in this DIY style. Oh, and the wallpaper was equally *magnifique.*

Colditz was a style all its own. The Cansot's

had gone to town in this little back room and wallpapered the ceiling, walls, the back of the door, the wardrobe door and even had a go at the window frames. Lock someone in that room for 24 hours and they might never recover. Our bedroom was done in a busy pattern, but liveable until you look at the unfaded bits where pictures had hung and it was pink and grey and green. Another psychotic nightmare. What they didn't wallpaper was painted a bilious greeny blue. All the décor could be fixed with a wall paper steamer and a lick of paint. It was do-able.

On the plus side…we didn't pay much for the house, it was in France, and it turned out that good French wine was only three Euros a bottle at *Super U*. Bonus.

As we cleaned and swept and tidied the house a few more treasures came to light. Trésor is such a nice word. Madame Marie and Madame Jeannine didn't want to work too hard or bend too far and so when I was vacuuming under the bed I found an old drawer full of photographs. They were real trésor. Old photos of weddings from the village. Relatives and so typically Breton style. There was old grandma with her Breton bonnet. Even older women with sour faces and men with whiskers and stout consitutions.

I wondered if they returned

Everyone was about 4ft tall. They were great to study. What lives those people must have led in their granite grey cottages, hunkered down into the earth.

We also found some medals awarded to Louis and a heap of old French coins. The French franc was once a currency with a long history.

There was also a tinted photograph of two sturdy looking soldiers. They must have gone to the First World War. I wondered if they returned

The sister's had not looked too hard or perhaps they gave up after they had raped, pillaged and plundered the good stuff. I closed the lounge room door and found Bernadette's *pantalon* (trousers) hanging behind the door. They were large and very short. I could now see why every door frame had a mark where her hands had, over the years, rubbed the paint right through at about the metre mark. By looking around I could trace her shuffling steps and where she held onto the frames to the bathroom, kitchen and bedroom. Bernadette had used her old clothes as rags. These rags were her old knickers. Not the nicest thing to find under the sink. And whose teeth were in the kitchen drawer? Surely Bernadette would have been buried with her teeth.

'Put them in the bin.'

'You pick them up,' I said.

'You found them,' Boomie passed the buck quite neatly. I should be used to dealing with dead people. I had worked in archaeology in England for over five years *digging up dead people*, as my children often explained to their school teachers. Boomie gave me a piece of paper and I wrapped the little suckers up and threw them in the bin.

On top of a wardrobe we found a silver service cutlery canteen. The sisters overlooked this treasure. No need to buy knives and forks or spoons although the dessert spoons were bloody enormous. For little Breton people they must have had big mouths, with or without teeth. It was a cutlery set of old with royal blue velvet lining and soup ladles, serving spoons and fine dessert forks. The more you use silver the better it becomes. I washed everything in boiling hot water and gave them a buff. We may not be rich, but when you can eat from silver, life isn't too bad.

The kitchen table could tell a tale or two. Over the years it had been scrubbed clean of the Formica pattern. It also had a mechanism to make it bigger. A very convoluted mechanism.

There were wooden pegs – extra arms - slots and positioning pins. I'm always up for a challenge and began to nut the thing out. It was a simple task of taking the top off and lifting the under arms and pulling out the pins and re positioning then into the arms at the desired length then slotting the top back on with its pegs. Easy peasy. I covered the top with a tablecloth. In France they have a habit of covering their tables with pattered plastic table cloths. The patterns are of the wallpaper variety. When we had viewed the house I took note of the plastic table cloth with red checks and pink roses. We had seen them at *Super U*. I nearly went continental, but Boomie stopped me just in time.

There was also a cabinet that held an old treadle Singer sewing machine. Either the sisters didn't know what it was, or it was just too heavy to take away. It still had thread in it that matched Bernadette's trousers and some pins in the tray. I wondered if it was worth a bob or two, but after looking on the internet it was just a curiosity. We put it where we could use it as a cupboard top.

The main piece of furniture in the kitchen was an old oak dresser. This had been Bernadette's main cupboard for years and all the inner shelves were bowed. The top three doors were inlaid with dimpled glass and the sideboard top had a big crack in it, but it had a rustic charm and was quite useful as the only cupboard in the kitchen. We took the top half off and found quite few francs that had slid under the shelf over the years. There was a well-worn track in the floor covering from the dresser to the sink and the table. Her life was unfolding before our eyes.

We also inherited a clock. This wall clock was in a carved wooden box with a silver pendulum and hung on the kitchen wall. Boomie wound it up and it began again after a few years of neglect. It has three winding keyholes and so Boomie did the lot. It had a chime ever quarter hour, the first chime at 15 minutes past is one of a 4-part tune. Then it strikes the hour. The village church also strikes the hour and can be heard quite plainly echoing up the hill. All things being equal they should chime at roughly the same time.

At first, having a chiming clock is quaint and new, but after a while it is just plain annoying. What became more annoying was that the clock, now christened Bernadette chimed whenever it felt like it. Four o'clock came at 1:15. 6:30pm is midnight. We had the shock of our lives at around 3am to hear the quarter hour chime, then ten o'clock then the three-quarter hour one after another. Other times it may go for 12 hours before it decides to chime. Boomie tried letting Bernadette wind down completely and just wound the clock. She worked well like this for perhaps a few days then one evening while we were having a wine she chimed 11 times – albeit very dilatory chimes and that was all. The most peculiar thing about Bernadette is that she keeps perfect time. A clock not to be trifled with and very strange *trésor* indeed.

But the real bonus was the boiler under the house. It was relatively new and the diesel tank that fed it still had a sizable amount of fuel in it. We would have hot water and be warm in winter.

Our little house was built partly into a rise and so the back was level with the grass, but the front was high off the ground. This made the underneath

102

as big as the house above. A great space for a car and motorbike. It also had a fireplace. I could see it as Boomie's man cave. All this area was an earth floor, beaten into submission over the years. And there was quite a lot of junk. Louis Cansot had collected stuff, all of it junk. Although if we wanted a walking frame in good condition it was there and we ummed and ahhed about the usefulness of our very own commode chair. Nothing like a second-hand commode chair to get the pulse racing. The main part of the shed was taken up with Bernadette's homemaking. She had, one upon a time, done quite a bit of preserving. We had shelves and shelves of glass jars and all the paraphernalia that goes with that enterprise. Everything was covered in dust and cobwebs. It would take quite a while to sort that lot out. There were a few discarded gardening tools and a wheelbarrow. Nothing had been touched, by the look of it, for about 30 years. Obviously the Cansot sisters didn't want to get their hands dirty.

We thought we had found all the surprises in the house. We were yet to tackle the overgrown garden.

Breton bonnets and clogs

Louis & Bernadette

13

Necessity is the mother of where all your troubles begin.

We had 8 weeks to whip the house into a viable liveable condition. We thought this would also be ample time for the OFII people to issue us with our necessary documents.

Our priority was to sort through what we wanted to keep and what we wanted to throw away. There was quite a bit on the latter side of the argument. What to do with all the old stuff was a bit of a problem. Perhaps we could order a skip and begin the clean-up. In Australia skips are all the rage. You get a big skip dropped off on your footpath and when it's full, a quick phone call and someone comes and takes it away. Problem solved. In France there is no such thing as a handy skip for the general public. When we asked Fabien, at the Carrosserie, about a skip she didn't have a clue. I drew a picture including the truck with the big hook, but it didn't ring any bells. Builders have them, but as for your ordinary Joe Blow or *Jacque Brun* it is as far out of the mainstream as asking for warm champagne.

The French have a certain reticence to throwing things away. We were told by the real estate agent that they never knock anything down, rather just let it decay. By the look of our house they were waiting for it to become an archaeological curiosity.

The other thing that was a bit of a priority was getting the boiler working for hot water. We had been having cold showers for a few days and the novelty was wearing thin. Fabien, was a real help. When I explained that we needed hot water she rang the plumber for me and arranged a time that very afternoon. She obviously thought it was unthinkable that we should suffer any longer.

Now I should point out that when doing up the boat we have had many and varied dealings with tradies. Boilermakers, sheet metal workers, carpenters, and shonky workmen have all been over our threshold. So when Fabien said 'that very afternoon', we put the kettle on and thought it might be sometime next week. Tradesmen or *artisans* are a law unto themselves.

Imagine our surprise when, within an hour, a van pulled up and a short, stout man hopped out and thrust his hand out for a handshake. He was as round as he was high, but he worked like dynamite. This wasn't the attitude we had been accustomed to with tradesmen. Usually they came, scratched their balls, took a phone call, had a think, went to the van, took a phone call, came back with their tools and then proceeded to talk about their weekend while you paid by the hour.

Our little plumber was a whirlwind of work. He got right to the nub of the problem and threw himself at the job with gusto. We watched fascinated as he fiddled about and then bent down to take a look at the innards of the beast that was our boiler.

'He must be an expert,' I said to Boomie. 'See,

he has a mighty powerful plumbers crack.' The mark of an *artisan*.

He must be an expert

We cautiously asked if he could speak English. '*Parlez vous Anglais?*'

'No.' It was a definitive answer albeit with a smile. He then began to chatter away in French and we just nodded and said,

'*Oui.*'

Our boiler was clogged, but with a few new spare filters the plumber pulled me over and showed me how to fire it up. It thrumped into life and that was it. He bled all the heaters throughout the house all the while explaining in French what he was going to do, and what he was doing, and what I should do in the future. I nodded a lot and watched. While we had a little man on the job I asked if he would take a look at our stove. He came upstairs and fiddled about for a bit and then said all was well and went back to packing up his tools. I could still smell gas and went downstairs to inform him.

I sniffed and pretended to light a match and then said,

'Boom.' It was instantly understood.

I didn't know someone of his stature could run that

fast. He bolted up the steps and turned everything off. Then carefully explained, very slowly in French that I must not use the stove. I think I got the idea.

'Kaput?' It was a German word, but it was all I could think of in the circs.

'Kaput.' He nodded. Just another thing that we bought with the house and had to throw away. We so needed a handy skip it wasn't funny.

He left his card and waved goodbye.

The bill would come in the post.

Hot water meant hot showers. Bliss.

Everyone wants to make a good impression with the neighbours. We got off to a good start by trashing the front yard. It began to look like a junk yard, all we needed was a junk yard dog and maybe a car body or two. The method in our madness was to amass a heap of stuff that was broken, useless or both. Somehow we would contract someone to take it all away. So we began to throw things out the door. It was mid throw of a particularly ugly snatch of telephone wires and cables that the neighbour waved to me. I threw my booty from the window onto the ground and waved back.

'*Bonjour.*'

'*Bonjour.*' We were off to a good start.

Myriam knew a fraction more English than I knew French. This is where google translate really works. So do hand gestures. It turned out that Myriam had a trailer and she was offering to take out junk to the dump. It was an offer too good to refuse.

I invited her over to see the amount of junk we had and swept my hands wide to take in all the preserving jars. It turned out her mother did that sort of thing and would take all the jars. We might even get some back with plums in them as our back yard had three plum trees that were prolific.

As we stood about in the front yard the conversation came around to Bernadette and Louis Cansot. Myriam had known Madame Cansot for quite a few years and filled us in on the gossip.

Madame Cansot was a feisty old woman. Very strong. Very opinionated according to Myriam. Louis had been dead many years and without a man about the house it fell into neglect. Bernadette was about 4ft tall and Myriam said she liked to eat. A polite way to saw she was overweight. There was plenty more we heard too. It seemed the sisters contracted a fellow to slash the grass. The grass was duly cut, but as payment the Cansot sisters said he could have the washing machine. That was nice of them considering we had bought it in the contract. This must have been early on in the contract, because the grass was thigh high once again.

The Cansot's had left their mark and now it was time for the Ashwins to breathe new life into the old house.

We just needed to get rid of the dross.

One thing that had a life of its own was the guttering arrangement at the side of the house. It had been broken for some time by the look of the mould stain on the stonework and all the water was making the house damp. We called in a gutter man and with efficiency he came with a ladder. We pointed, made drawings on his notebook and pointed some more. He was more than happy to give us a quote. And while I had him on the spot I asked if we might put his ladder to use to see what was in the loft. A great many French houses have a loft with a hobbit looking door stuck up in the air. There is no way to get to the door except by a ladder. I was hoping for Nazi loot in the loft. Boomie thought there might be old things stored from long ago. The gutter man went up first and tried the door. It wasn't locked. He came down and I shot up like a rat up a drainpipe. When there is Nazi loot to find, I'm not one to hang back.

The area was remarkably clean. We had new-ish insulation batts, and there wasn't a skerrick of treasure to be seen. What we did have were two little bowls and a cracked plate. Strange that they should be up there. Were they left over from the crazy cousin locked in the attic? Were they for the resistance fighter? I grabbed them and brought them down. Boomie went up and being ever practical took a good look at our roof and our electrical systems. It was all do-able.

'More junk?' he asked as he watched me wash the bowls.

'Utilitarian objects.'

We also asked the gutter man to take a look at

our well. We didn't know we had one until I moved a piece of corrugated iron. It is more of a holding tank made of cement than a well, but it had a big ol' antique hand pump to bring the water up. This pump was seized solid, but the unfortunate thing about the whole arrangement was that if we took the pump away the water from the tank would flood under the house. Our gutter man scratched his head and then shrugged. It was well beyond his pay grade to give an opinion. The pump would stay.

When you begin to put your mark on a house the first thing that needs to be done is move furniture around. We had 4 huge wardrobes which I could see needed to be swapped around in the rooms. The oldest one would make a decent bookcase. We just had to get it from Colditz to the lounge room. First, we needed to move the bed to make room. The mattress was a lumpy thing that didn't want to bend around the tight corner. We twisted, bent, and swore but it didn't want to go. If we couldn't get a bendy(ish) mattress out the door there was no way we'd get the old oak wardrobe. How they got it in the room in the first place would remain a mystery. The window looked too small, and the doorway was out of the question. It would just need to stay put. When you sit on the toilet you can see it and even to a man with one eye it has a decided lean backwards. I think Louis, at some point, cut off the back legs 2cm shorter just for the hell of it. It is like an optical illusion. You are never quite sure if you are sitting straight, the wall is falling inward or the wardrobe in about to topple over. The other wardrobes were just as hard to move. They came

112

apart in three sections, but over the years they had fused together and because the doors were narrow and small to each room, they would just stay put. We'd work around them until we'd buy a book case or figure a way to prise them apart. So pretty much everything stayed as it was originally.

It was a wonderment to our neighbour, Myriam how two Australians could ever find their way to her little village and buy a house.

'The internet is a marvellous thing,' I said.

Myriam said she was glad we had bought the house and asked,

'Do you like the rain?'

14

One man's trash is another man's treasure.

Because twilights seem to last forever in the Northern Hemisphere we could work right up to about 7.30 and then we were wacked. Our pile of junk grew as we tossed those Breton pillows, the fridge, stove, a couple of broken chairs and that hideous broken light fitting onto the pile. Then we really got serious.

The front door, (there wasn't a back door – I know we baulked at the other house without one, but well…), didn't open fully and it was difficult to get all the stuff to the steps for the heave ho. The problem was the vinyl floor covering in the kitchen. It was rucking up and stopping the door. The solution was to pull it out.

It's very satisfying to grab a big portion of old vinyl and rip it to bits. It gives a substantial gggrrrrrhhhhhhhtttt as you put your back into it. I got to work and was chucking stuff out the window like an expert…sans *artisan* crack and we found another vinyl floor covering underneath. This one was old by the look of the wear pattern from the dresser to the sink. I got to work pulling this up to discover another layer underneath. No effort was involved when they laid the new coverings. The original one had some sort of horse hair underlay and it was holding onto the floorboards like a Titanic survivor to a life ring. There was no ripping this sucker up. It came away in small crumbs until Boomie employed Mr Crowbar. He would start with a small corner and then I would pull. Most of the awful patterned stuff came away, but the horsehair remained. The whole floor was now covered in horrid looking stuff like old pubic hair. Now the door swung open like a drunk. Of course, the front yard mountain looked even worse. All we needed was mattress to complete the ensemble.

There was a mattress we needed to throw, but it was too good to chuck. It was a new looking plastic covered single bed for old people's complaints.

On our nightly walks we had been past an old folk's home. Perhaps they would like it and the commode and the walker. A job lot for nothing. All they needed to do was collect it.

No matter how much we love demolishing stuff, we are always up for an outing. We downed tools and went in search of an answer. It turned out the home knew Madame Cansot.

'*Oui. Merci.*' They were happy to take our cast offs.

It was easy, albeit with hand signals and drawings. There was no way I was going to do a Marcel Marceau and mime using a commode chair. Some things are better left to google translate.

Myriam came good with her promise of the trailer. We expected an Australian size 6x4ft with hungry boards. Myriam has a trailer that might have been pulled by a Barbie dolls motorhome and horse float. It was tiny by Aussie standards. It was

116

obvious we would be making several trips to the dump. The other thing that was pretty self-evident was that if we were going to get anything in the dinky toy trailer it would need to be in reasonably small bits. A stove just wouldn't fit, and as for a fridge…

It's not often you get to really smash things up with a lump hammer, a crowbar and brute force. It is oddly satisfying. Myriam stood by grabbing the odd thing that she couldn't do without while the Ashwins went to town.

'Do you want any *meubles*?' I asked Myriam.

She looked at me askew.

'*Meubles?* (furniture)' I said in my best French.

'*Ah, meubles.*' Myriam said. Then she explained I was asking if she wanted some men's balls and did a little mime to get the point across. It's all in the pronunciation apparently.

We piled all we could in the trailer and then Boomie went to the dump with Myriam. The back seat was taken up with junk so I was left behind.

Boomie came back in due course and waxed lyrical about the French and their dump, called *la Déchetterie.*

'The dump man kissed me,' Boomie said. This never happened in Australia. Myriam knew everyone and it seemed a friend of Myriams was a friend of ours. Boomie told me about the French and their rubbish.

The Kiss

I had to see for myself.

La Déchetterie is a very ordered affair. There are 4 very large skips each one taking a different type of rubbish. Green waste, building materials, metal and plastic. The French take their rubbish seriously. They sort scrupulously. They also have an area for paper, glass and polystyrene, batteries, electrical goods, white goods and the like. The man comes out of his little office and once you tell him what you have, he points you in the right direction.

Myriam was very kind, but we felt we couldn't keep asking for her trailer, so we decided to go it alone.

At first the dump man was a little suspicious of us and would hover over our dumping procedure. But after a few trips he was confident we knew what we were doing. The sight that took a bit more getting used to, was us walking to the dump with our wheelbarrow full of stuff.

I should point out the Ashwins have been going to the dump in Australia for about 20 years or more. I don't know why, but we always have stuff to throw away. It is a standing joke that Boomie takes me to the dump on my birthday, such is the nature of our regular visits. Bringing our habit to France just seemed the natural thing to do.

In Australia once you have deposited your rubbish, marvelled at the ibis and pelicans scavenging and seen the plastic rubbish bags blown onto the wire fence in odd shapes you drive away holding your nose with the windows wound up so you don't swallow a fly. In France once you have off loaded you are required to clean up if you have dropped anything. They have a plethora of brooms, shovels, and dustpans for everyone to do the right thing. I saw a woman pick up a dustpan and broom to sweep a few grass cuttings from the tarmac. The dump man thanks you and shakes your hand or, in Boomie's case, gives the Breton three kisses on the cheek. We felt almost family.

What happens to the food rubbish is a testament to how the French behave. I previously thought someone had stolen our wheelie bin, but this was not the case. The French municipality and Government in general have the idea that the citizenry, given the right environment and circumstances, will do the right thing. And so they do.

In every corner of the village there are large wooden crates and taller wooden boxes with shutes in them. These are for household rubbish. But it gets better. The local *Mairie* (council) provide free of charge large yellow plastic bags for us to sort our rubbish. All the packaging – and the French go to town on packaging – goes in this yellow bag, then in the crate. They even come with a handy bit of string to tie them up. Food scraps and the like go in black plastic then through the hatch to the larger box. It's all very civilized. Then a truck comes around and lifts the whole contraption up and empties it by separating the two halves of the box. Where it goes I don't know, but who cares. No-one abuses the system by putting – for instance old vinyl floor covering in bags or half a broken chair, because *la Déchetterie* is free and every village has one. It is a system that works. There is no cursing and swearing because someone forgot to put the bin out and therefore it must sit for another week festering and breeding maggots.

We buy small 20 litre black plastic bags, which are as cheap as chips, and every day on our way out to the shops drop off our waste. How simple is that. Naturally this service needs to be paid for via taxes, but we were assured by Myriam that they are not astronomical. We kept our finger's cross she was correct.

The other thing *la Déchetterie* has is a shipping container for the 'good' stuff. You know, all the stuff that is too good to throw away. This is my heaven.

120

'Now don't go bringing more stuff back than we have dropped off.' Boomie was always saying things like this.

'It's just recycling,' I said.

The French might not have very good taste in wallpaper, but they have 'ordinarily' really good junk. I started simple with a couple of wine glasses. Essentials! The shipping container was full of books, 1970s kitchen gadgets – even the French it seems cannot go past a flip-o-matic recipe holder, clothes, baby cots, mountains of crockery and some very odd looking ornaments. Who in their right mind would go to Bordeaux for a holiday and come back with a plastic cactus toothpick holder toast rack. They were also big on things with a clog theme. I had a light fitting that would fit right in.

As the day progressed I came back with brandy balloons, more wine glasses, a bedside table and a trivet. Not that I drank brandy or had been hankering for a trivet since my 21st birthday party, but it's kinda irresistible. Quickly Boomie said that the rule was we could only take if we were dumping at the same time. I began to look around for things to throw away.

With all the major things taken with Myriam's goodwill we only had to contend with the old wood stove. This was made of cast iron, had about a dozen fire bricks in it and wouldn't fit through the door.

Myriam said her friend might take it, but we said he would only be taking it in bits as it was too big.

Boomie got to work dismantling it in the kitchen.

Handy hint # Don't ever try to get soot out of a pubic hair floor. It was not a pretty sight. The stove was taken apart one small agonising piece at a time and although it was hard work it was interesting to see how it was made in the first place. Sturdy, solid, but amazingly the screws, nuts and bolts still turned. Well some of them anyway. And it was a heavy as lead…and we knew about lead having got rid of 153kg of lead from the ballast in the boat.

With most of the thing dismantled it was time to heft the carcass down the stairs. Not easy, but one step at a time and our backs screaming we rolled it to the front yard. There was no way in the world we could begin to lift it to the trailer and so Boomie went to work smashing it. It ate the lump hammer and spat out the pieces. Cast iron is remarkably tough. Boomie took to it with Mr Crowbar. Levers always work better than brute force. Piece by piece it broke and we loaded it to the trailer.

Next to go were all the rotten shelves under the house. Myriam's mother came over and there was more kissing before she took all the jars.

She was intrigued by these 'can do' Australians and chatted away in French.

It turned out Myriam's mother (grandma) knew the Cansots and so I fetched the old wedding photos for her to take a look. She pointed out who was who and saw a few familiar faces in the crowd. The old Breton women in their clogs and bonnets made her smile with a certain pride. She didn't know who the soldiers were, but gave us some insights into the Cansot family. She said Bernadette was a great one for preserving. It is *de rigueur* in Brittany. This brought us neatly back to the jars. Grandma packed them away in her car and we were left with the bare shelves.

The wooden shelves were a very shoddy homemade affair and falling to bits. They practically fell down with one swing of Mr Crowbar. By the end of the day we had managed to get rid of so much stuff we wondered if we had paid too much for the house as most of its guts were now at *la Déchetterie.*

We only had the floor coverings left to throw away. They would wait for another day.

On the up side we now had wine glasses, a trivet and a couple of woven baskets. You can never have too many woven baskets.

'Hettie…'

'What?'

15

The French way.

The French have a certain mindset that needs to be understood. Not that they are very different than the rest of the world, but more in the nature of

'This is the way we do it and this is the way it will be done.'

We waited anxiously for OFII to send us a letter. Every day I waited for the postman to drop a letter in our box. I thought I might make it easier for him and went about trimming the hedge that had overtaken the box. Then I discovered that we didn't have the regulation blue number on our house. Best to make it super easy for the postman. The French are very particular about their regulations.

Your letter box must be regulation size and if you look throughout the village everyone has one or two of the designs allowed. They should be a regulation height too although we have seen a few variations on this theme. They also should lock. That way the post cannot be accused of anything untoward. We had a regulation box, but as for a house number …

All houses have a small metal square on their fence with blue background and white number.

Ours was missing. The obvious thing to do was ask the *Mairie* for a new one. So armed with a google translated sentence or two we went in search of a number 50.

It was easier than expected. The woman at the *Mairie* understood our problem and said she would ring us when it arrived. The only thing we had to contend with was a phone call conducted entirely in French. The only thing that flummoxed her was that it was missing in the first place. Unthinkable!

While we waited for our all-important OFII we decided to take a few trips to the dump ourselves. Thinking ahead we had shipped over our folding bikes and now we loaded these aluminium work horses up with stuff and walked them about 20 minutes down the hill. I quickly learnt to take my large backpack for the return trip. Over the next week I amassed a dinner service that might have fed a banquet at Versailles. I had plates with gold rims, bowls with flowers painted on them, two large soup terrines, dessert bowls and heaps of different style glasses. All for free. It was getting to the stage where Boomie would start riding back without me, such was my fervour. Our two of everything became 14 of everything. Then I picked up a French cook book written in English. It was all I needed to get excited about cooking in France. The dump man was intrigued at my enthusiasm, but he never stopped me, so I figured as long as I was dumping, I was allowed to shop. I also brought back small pieces of furniture that were in keeping with the old house. Slinging a small table over your handlebars turns out to be the easiest thing in the world.

Explaining to your husband that it is a vital part of infrastructure takes a bit more thought. In the end I think I picked that shipping container clean of anything worth having. Now I would just hunt for things that I 'really' needed.

We were getting into the swing of things in France and the French way quite nicely. Realistically we just had to remember that nothing happens between the hours of 12 and 2. Lunch is sacrosanct. If anything happened on a Monday it would be a miracle. Banks shut on a Monday. The *Boulangerie* shut on a Monday and the library didn't open until Wednesday. Workmen started at 9am and not a minute before and then there was the issue of payment. *Artisans* are, we have found, in no hurry for their money. We needed to chase up the plumber to pay our bill and then the lovely woman behind the desk had to ask our plumber what the price might be. It all happens in good time they say as they wave away the problem with a pragmatic air and a shrug of their shoulders.

France might look like it is in the twenty first century, but in a small village they aren't quite there yet. There is no paywave. Everyone, well almost everyone, pays by cheque.

When we applied for our mortgage we were sent a cheque book. That quaint old fashioned thing that I hadn't used since the 1970s. Tradesmen or *artisans* typically in the village don't take credit cards or debit cards. They take cheques. I had a steep learning curve writing the numbers in French. At *Super U* all the women write cheques or get the checkout woman to print it. In Australia we would be tearing our hair out as we waited.

The other thing that is an anomaly is the way they have an inordinate amount of patience. At *Super U* everyone waits as the 4ft, 80 year old woman packs her trolley after she has paid. We all just watch her put one thing in at a time. French supermarkets have done away with plastic shopping bags and so it is either just pack the goods back into the trolley or into baskets brought from home or *Super U* bags. It can sometimes take up to 8 minutes for the customer to leave the check out. Everyone just patiently waits.

But what they don't do when they wait is talk to one another. At home in Port Douglas, or anywhere for that matter people chat when in line. In France everyone is stoically quiet. We tried to have a bit of a conversation about the weather, but it soon became obvious that it is not the done thing.

The French are ultra-polite. I cannot speak for the whole country, but the places and people we have met have validated this statement. Over the years standards have slipped so social historians tell us, but Boomie and I still find their politeness a refreshing change from the grab and go culture of Australia. They will always greet you on the street with a *bonjour.* I like that. Even when advertising on the supermarket noticeboard to give away a cot or cat they start their ad with *bonjour.* If they are in a car they will nod in your direction.

'*Bonjour, Monsieur et Madame,*' they say as we pass them on the street.

'*Bonjour,*' we reply.

And it is the same with goodbyes. When the French say

'*A bientôt,*' (see you soon) they sound like they mean it.

We can't speak French, but that doesn't stop people from speaking to us in slow and precise French so that we might understand. They take the time and the trouble to try to make us understand.

And they are effusive once they get to know you. Grabbing your arm, going out of their way to shake your hand and that sort of thing, which may or may not include kissing.

Australians are particularly welcome in our bit of France. Boomie's Akubra hat garners a few double takes on the street. The English have a slightly less warm reception. When we mention we are from Australia we are either seen as some sort of crazy wild adventurers or the Frenchman is just glad we are not English. Australia is seen as 'the' exotic destination.

I love shopping for new and different ingredients. But what gets me every time is the way the French package things. If you want sweet patisseries then they come in a box of three. I'm not sure if this is a clever marketing strategy to make you buy more than you need or it has some other significance. If you are a family of four then you will need to buy two boxes. If you are a family of two then you can either fight for the one left or give in gracefully. Pork chops come in packets of seven or nine. It is the same with sausages. Haven't they heard of round figures? Just the French way.

Food is a little different to the normal Australian meat and three veg. The French have a love affair

128

with chocolate and put it in everything. There are all sorts of breads with chocolate in them. There are cakes with chocolate on and in them. There are three shelves in the supermarkets dedicated to dark chocolate. Their other love is dairy products. The cold section of *Super U* is chocka block full of yogurt, cheese, butter and the all-important cream. Learning about the various creams could take me a lifetime, but I'm willing to invest the time to get to know how to cook with cream. They have fresh cream, sour cream, semi thick cream, semi thick for sauce cream, cream for béchamel sauce and cream just for the hell of having cream. The choice of butter is not far behind the choice of cream.

Cheese is on a whole nuther level. We set ourselves the task of trying a different cheese every time. Some were mild, smooth and creamy (naturally). Some had a bit of a bite. And then we bought a cheese that smelt like a bit of hedgehog roadkill. It was pretty disgusting. So much so that we had to throw it away. I like cheese, but even this tested my palate. It made the house stink, the cupboard pong and I won't even go there about the end product in the loo. It was foul. The tricky part was we didn't keep the wrapper and

couldn't remember what it looked like. And if you thought about it for a minute, Madame Antoinette didn't say let them eat stinky cheese. We decided to stick to cheese we could pronounce.

Stick to cheese we could pronounce

And on the subject of all things stinky, the French have a sort of love/hate relationship with their dogs. The French dogs we have met have a very continental attitude. That is to say they, quite likely, hate everyone. No matter that we see the dogs in our street every day and give them a friendly *'bonjour'* they snarl and bark When we are going for an evening walk every dog behind a fence wants to fight. How brave they would be on the other side of the fence we have yet to ascertain. We set off a chain of barking right down the street. And to top the whole thing off the French have never heard of a pooper scooper – well I can only speak for our village. Barker's nests are an ever-present danger. We met a woman who wanted to tell us about how she learnt English as a girl in the war and all the while her small white mutt squatted at our gate and showed us what he was eating the day before. Then with a

'A bientôt,' she walked on, oblivious to the nest her dog left behind.

130

'Merci Beaucoup Madame!'

There is one other thing that puts France in a different league than Australia and that is Sunday. Sunday in Australia is for mowing the lawn, doing the garden, barbeques, washing the car and the usual Sunday chores. In France Sunday is for nothing. No-one arcs up a power tool.

No-one tinkers with the car or gets the line trimmer going. Sunday is for serious peace and quiet.

We found this a bit strange on our first few Sundays and Boomie said he would line trim when someone one else started. We waited all day in vain. The streets are silent. Around 5 or 6 when the twilight is in full swing people come out and promenade down the street, walking their dogs, depositing rubbish and chatting, but as for putting their back into it and getting their hands dirty, it just doesn't happen…and of course Monday is a write off.

The other thing the French take seriously is their bread. Someone told me that the basic baguette recipe is set by law – woe betide anyone who tampers with a staple like bread. Even if it isn't true, being France, it sounds like it should be. Riots have happened over bread. Revolutions have taken place over bead. Don't mess with the French when it comes to bread.

Marie Antoinette said

'Let them eat cake.' I think she knew a thing or two about the dietary habits of her fellow French. They have more cakes per head of population than anywhere on the continent…except Vienna. The Viennese really know their cakes.

French bread is typically the crusty variety, unless it has chocolate in it. In fact bread is either *avec* (with) chocolate or *sans* (without) chocolate as far as I can see.

A baguette is great the minute it's baked. Warm and fluffy on the inside. *Pain* (bread) in different shapes is terrific when fresh. The French buy their bread twice a day to enjoy the experience. Who wouldn't? Six hour old baguettes are like rock. They would test the jaw of a crocodile. The crust becomes so brittle I have drawn blood on the roof of my mouth trying to eat it. Of course the French don't do anything as crass as eat day old bread, but the Ashwins are made of more economical stuff. I have grated it for breadcrumbs, made croutons, soaked it in soup and made garlic bread, but there is just so much you can do with six inches of hard baguette.

To be fair there are sliced breads on offer at the shops and *boulangerie,* but these don't last long either. On the plus side the bread is *sans* preservatives and all the nasty stuff and it's cheap. So the only thing to do is to adopt the French way and buy every day or – unthinkable in France – go without.

'You don't eat bread?' Myriam asked. It was beyond her level of comprehension that life or a meal could exist without a baguette.

It was like,

'What, you mean to say you dig a hole and bury it.'

'*Mon Dieu.*' (My God!)

Although the French have a style all their own, they sometimes come up with something that is so thought through, so simple a design and so easy to use it should be right up there for a medal.

I'm talking door and window hinges.

I don't exactly know if the French invented them, but I will give them the credit anyway. In Australia a hinge is a set piece of metal, six holes and joined at the hip so that

hanging a door you need to get all your checkouts and holes just right. It is a tricky business. In France door and window hinges are simple. One side, ie the door, has a female little receptacle like a bullet casing and the other side has the male pin. So you just lift and separate or lift and position and it pops into place. If you wanted you could take all the doors and windows off in ten minutes or less. I was so enamoured by the hinges I wanted to do it for the hell of it.

But whereas they do hinges well, their ideas on brooms are dismal.

I like a broom I can push. Therefore, its bristles need to be raked in such a fashion so as they can gather the dirt in front. The French have the silly idea that you pull the pile of dirt towards you. Therefore. the bristles are straight up and down. It also means that you can never get a good action going unless you sweep towards your slippers.

If I try to push my French broom it just refuses

to sweep and begins to flick my pile to the next room.

'In France we pull.' And that is that. They also sell brooms the wicked witch of the west might want for her birthday. Brush stalks bound together. These are for paths etc. I've seen housewives using them to great effect. These have a side to side swinging motion so your feet don't get dirty. There is still a great division of labour in the village. The women still do the housework, the men the garden and most of the chatting over the fence. Every morning we'd see women sweeping and cleaning wearing their housecoats. I though housecoats went out with the 50s, but not here. I was feeling a bit French myself and for a moment I contemplated getting one too. They are practical, sensible for saving your clothes and come in bright colours with big pockets.

'You will look ridiculous,' Boomie said. I probably would at that.

One other thing that that I have found to be really clever is envelopes. The packet I purchased have gum on one side so you can peel them off like notepaper. No more cascading envelopes in the drawer or on the table. Other places might have them, but I've never seen them before. Such a simple idea that works well.

Somehow all these things just slowly crept into our psyche and we slipped effortlessly (well almost) into being French. I started with cheese, cream and chocolate. Boomie went for a cheeky red.

But one of the French people's most endearing qualities is their friendliness. They will always have a smile for you, just don't try to disturb them during lunch.

16

The Louis way.

After doing up a boat and owning a few houses of our own, Boomie and I thought we knew a thing or two about renovations. Living in hardware stores every weekend you are bound to pick up a few handy hints.

Louis Cansot didn't frequent hardware stores very often. I say this with an expert eye.

Our little house had more than a few battle scars. Most of them inflicted by Louis. He wasn't a handyman's &^%$hole, as Boomie so succinctly put it.

'They are just a bit quirky,' I said.

The tiles in the kitchen for the splashback were a prime example. Boomie saw right away they needed to come off. Some weren't even attached to the wall, but just sort of hanging there. When laying tiles there is an expectation that you will get them in a straight line. Louis didn't worry about all that. These square white tiles were very higgledy piggledy. The wall at some point had been plastered and then a coating of cement was added. The cement was like a BMX bike track and Louis had just tiled over everything. It was a lesson in what not to do with plain tiles. When he came to the redundant electrical socket he hammered out a small square of tile and stuck it in with his eyes closed. Boomie spent a good two days taking all the tiles off. What we were left with was a badly rendered cement wall over ancient plaster which we found was about 4 inches thick.

The plaster was another problem. Bernadette and Louis liked nothing better than to hang a picture or two about the place. It makes it look homely. Except with plaster so thick the nails have nothing to hang onto and they fall out…sooner rather than later. So what did Louis do? He just repeated the same procedure. One particularly hideous picture of a donkey hauling tomatoes up a street in Spain had 12 nail holes in the plaster. I would have given up by nail hole two. Louis and Bernadette were made of sterner stuff.

We quickly began to use the vernacular,
'Louis had a hand in this.' And 'Another Louis special.' He was something else.

Being the handyman *extraordinaire* Louis went all out with the electrics. In France people can wire their own house and then call in an expert to sign off on their work. Louis obviously didn't have the telephone number of the electrician. The first thing we found was that the earth strap to the house was an old bit of pipe with a wire attached in an extremely haphazard way. It was barely there and downright dangerous. We re-attached and hoped for the best until we could engage an electrician. The

138

house had had many incarnations of switches. Each new one was just tacked on under the old ones, which sometimes hung out of the wall cavity like drunken sailors on a light pole, and a bit of wire patched into the mains. Some of the switches were too big and so Louis hammered out a bit of door frame to make them fit. A stylish solution. The toilet light was a classic. The old wire was cut and just hanging about, and the new light was patched in half was down the wire to the switch with a couple of screws. None of the wire are in the walls as the house has solid stone walls so they all run either through the ceiling or along the skirting boards and up the door frames. Because the Cansot's were so small all the switches are around 1.5 metres from the floor. All this is liveable for the moment, but the spooky thing is that the light switches sometimes don't work, sometimes they work on their own and sometimes they spark when you turn them on. It's a bit hit and miss.

Another Louis classis solution was installing the bathroom suite. Most people would attached the hand basin to the wall, fix the taps so they don't move and get the drainage working like it should. Louis had been more inventive. Our hand basin was free standing and to make it level he had inserted a wooden wedge at the pedestal top. To get it right he inserted a few more. They look like old teeth sticking out under the basin. The taps are held in with little bits of rubber and the drain plug is a bit of old pipe that leaks. It has a way of growing on you as you clean it and I use one of the wedges to hang my cleaning cloth so it is sort of handy. The shower tray was a corker.

The main problem with the tray is that it is not supported under the house. It just hangs by the merest lip, cemented in with a hope and a prayer. A builder came around to take a look and all Mark could say was,

'That's a bit different.' A Louis special. Of course the tiles in the bathroom have had the same care and attention lavished on them as in the kitchen. And they are a repeat pattern that could only be French. The toilet tiles, we found, were stuck onto wallpaper and so had no hope of staying there permanently. Most people read the paper in the loo, we picked off the old tiles and then the wallpaper. It pays to be productive with every moment of your day!

What wasn't tiled was painted or wallpapered. Louis liked dark colours. When you have a small house, it's just the thing apparently in France to try to make it smaller by painting it in dark brown. Not a spec of magnolia to be seen. And he went to town with a dark wood pvc contact that in Australia we often use to line a drawer or cover a school book. This was stuck halfway down the wall and when it came off half the plaster came with it.

'Nothing that can't be fixed,' Boomie said as I stood with a hunk of plaster the size of a large suitcase in my hand.

We also had what looked like a transformer on the kitchen wall that was an old gas water heater. It had ceased to be useful years ago and now stood like a redundant robot. Louis hadn't bothered to disconnect it and the water tap was jammed in the on position. We would need to get our plumber back for the disconnection. I painted two eyes on it to give it a bit of character while it waited.

All this sounds like a nightmare, but it was only a matter of elbow grease and a bit of paint to make it sparkle again. So far we didn't find anything that was uber major in the way of structural. Well except for the gaps in the wooden floorboard and the fireplace downstairs. This had been put together before Louis had discovered you need more than mortar to stick bricks. Cement works well. Boomie was leaning on it and it collapsed like a Roman ruin.

The gaps in the floor were another matter altogether.

Our floor was wooden planks over oak beams. The beams rested on stone outer walls. So basically it's a square of stone and wooden beams straddling across to support the internal walls and the floor. There is one large concrete beam holding the whole shebang together. Over the years the wooden beams have sagged and this has the effect of lowering the floor in the middle of the house and the floor on the stone walls has remained at the pre sag level. Everything tends to run to the middle of the house. The beams are strong, they have been doing their job for over 70 years and are stable. It's just that you sometimes feel like you are walking uphill or sliding off your chair. If I put something on the kitchen table, like an egg, it needs to be anchored otherwise, it often ends up on the floor. I lost two eggs while making a cake as I turned my back for a moment.

It's quirky, but it's ours, it was cheap and it's in France. We have added to this that it probably won't be our last house in France.

On our walk to *super U* we pass number 5. This house is solid stone. It has those tiny little windows in the roof and a cute little garage on the side. I've always wanted a holly tree and number 5 has one. You can see where this is going. I can see myself with a studio/study with a desk under one of those little windows. I don't think Louis has had a hand in number 5 anywhere. That makes it attractive. I had a look on the internet and we now know it has been for sale for about 2 years. Practically begging for a new owner and would be a bargain. It's a tempting thought.

'We better get our OFII sorted first,' I said to Boomie.

I looked to the letter box, which was the only thing Louis hadn't had his hands on and willed our visa to come.

17

Tilling the soil is a noble occupation.

As May turned into June the days warmed up and we headed for the longest day of the year. Our thought naturally turned to the garden. I had heard that the French like to go natural with their gardens and they often let them revert to meadow. We had a more than a meadow. We had a wild untamed beast.

France blossoms in spring and the natives go to town with flowers. Even the sides of the road were blooming with wildflowers. Every colour, style and shape imaginable could be found. Boomie and I would stroll around the village and we were afflicted with garden envy. Our neighbours were particularly good at gardening. Hedges were trimmed perfectly, lawns cut immaculately and the profusion of flowers was dazzling. Some gardens had old wells or solid granite drinking troughs planted with cascading flowers. The commune had planter boxes on every wall and window sill. I began to make a mental list of the plants I would like to grow.

Every evening Boomie and I would take our wine out into our yard and discuss what we were going to do. We were full of grand plans, wonderful ideas and lush plantings. It was just the execution that was lacking. It looked like a lot of work. We had said we didn't want too much garden in our criteria, but as just about every other thing on the list had gone out the window, the garden was just another thing we convinced ourselves would be good fun, an opportunity for some exercise and it had been 11 years since we put our foot on a shovel.

We were drinking a dry red one evening thinking on the vegetable garden we could have when a young man of middle-eastern appearance came through the gate and handed us a pamphlet and smiled. He swept his hands wide to our 'garden' and said in halting French that he could cut. We looked at this angel from heaven, and the 4 expectant faces in his truck and thought all our troubles would be over.

'How much?' was the only question we needed to ask. He called his friends into our yard and they conversed as we went around with our imaginary chainsaw cutting down the old stumps, the dead trees, pulling the blackberries from the fence, slashing the grass and getting them to take it all away.

The Arab scratched his head and put a figure on paper. I wasn't quite sure what I was reading and so re-wrote the figure so there would be no mistake.

He nodded. He wanted all our savings. I wanted to ask him if he wanted a kidney as well. I almost caved in as I saw a veggie garden, roses and a wisteria walk, but I snapped out of it and said

'*No.*' There was a lot of jabbering and pointing and they went into a huddle then came back with another price.

'*No.*' More conversing and then a figure was

printed on the paper that we could all live with… just about anyway. They would start tomorrow he said.

'High five Boomie.' We were going to get a garden and all we needed to do was pay. How easy was that? My back was already thanking me.

The Arabs were true to their word and arrived bright and early with two trucks and another two men. They had all the tools and went to work slashing and cutting. As we had already agreed a price I tried to add just a bit more work here and there. What was an extra ten minutes to the job? Those Arabs worked like demons uncovering the washing line, the plum trees and other features we didn't know we had. Every so often there would be a shout,

'*Madame.*' I was being summoned. The main man would then point to a branch, a bush, a trailing rose and ask what I wanted done with it.

I'm pretty good at split second decisions when I need to be and I just drew my finger across my throat. That was all the boys needed in the way of the go ahead. Their chain saws did the rest.

There were a few haircuts that I hadn't sanctioned, but I could live with their haircut on the pampas grass and their efforts at topiary on a bay tree.

At the end of the day they all trooped upstairs and I used my cheque book to pay. It was the easy part, yet painful, as I watched our saving shrink by quite a considerable sum.

Depending on our mood and how our finances are travelling we either love or hate the Arabs. They

146

took our money, but they did take all the cuttings away, and we couldn't have done it by ourselves, but they were expensive, but it was three truckloads and six people. It all depends on which was the wind blows on the day. The more we looked at our 800 square metres the more we realised the Arabs were a necessary evil.

Now we could see what we had in the lay of the land. The topography was a sloping grassed area to the house. Just the thing for all the water to drain to the footings and make Colditz even colder. We also had a half hidden slate path of sorts that followed the washing line. The first thing we needed to do was rake up the left over grass. We made a list of things to do and poured another wine.

Of course having grand ideas, you need tools. The Ashwins subscribe to the maxim that if you want a good job you need good tools. We had inherited a wheelbarrow and a cement trowel. We needed more.

The wheelbarrow was pressed into service straight away as I scooped up grass and Boomie emptied it. I heard him shout,

'Hettie, have a look at this.'

The French have some weird ideas. The barrow, when tipped up, fell into bits. The sides, base and front just lay on the ground and all Boomie was left with was a frame and a flat tyre.

'I didn't do anything. Just ridiculous,' he said as he scratched his head. We took a look at this antique, cursing Louis, but it turns out that quite a lot of barrows are built like this. For what reason only the French can know. They are useless for tipping in the usual fashion. I perfected a rhythm all my own. I would pull a side off and use it as a sort of scoop. It wasn't elegant, but it worked.

We soon discovered the Cansots were pretty darn lazy. They threw their fire ash in a heap quite close to the door, and as for bottle caps, they were in a two metre radius from the top step and when we dug and raked we found about a million of them. Louis had a powerful thirst, or maybe it was Madame Cansot. When we were cleaning the fireplace which was boarded up we found a stash of booze. The Cansot sister's missed that one. There was an unopened bottle of rum. It was, by the label, 34 years old. In France often the drink of choice is *Pastis de Marseille*, an *aperitif anise*. We had gained an unopened bottle of this too. Someone in the Cansot family liked a tipple.

There was also a lifetime of sweet wrappers. Aluminium foil doesn't degrade at all, neither does cellophane, and Bernadette liked lollies. Peppermints, butterscotch, and fruit flavours littered the ground. She had a rather large sweet tooth, if she had any teeth left.

The other thing we found while we cleaned and made tentative efforts at a garden bed were coins. It was quite the archaeological dig. There were old Francs and centimes and we unearthed a one Franc aluminium coin 1945. *Trésor* galore. There was a moment when we sat back on our muddy heels and dreamed ourselves into the millions with a rare coin. We'd have an expert come and confirm it and then we'd find a Roman villa on our property, the government would pay us out to the tune of one hundred thousand and we could buy number 5 and live on Rue de Easy.

'Snap out of it.'

I quickly went to the internet to see if our booty was worth anything. Nup. They were about as rare as fresh air. I found another 'coin' that if it was cleaned I was sure it had a Roman Emperor's head on it. I had the fever for treasure hunting. Our house was at the beginning of a Roman Road so it was quite possible. It turned out to be one of Louis's buttons.

'Probably a fly button,' Boomie said.

'Always the voice of reason.'

What we did find that was useful was the head of an axe. It turns out Boomie has always had a hankering to own an axe. A man thing I guessed. So we cleaned it up and bought a handle and he went to work chopping up things. It reminded me of the old adage,

The best axe I have ever had. Only had two new handles and three new heads.

I found a grubber that was just my size. So we bought another handle and called it the lady grubber. Bernadette had thrown away old crockery in the garden and this was unearthed with the sieve we purchased. I began collecting the shards.

'Junk?' Boomie asked.

'No. I just wanted to keep them.'

'Why?'

'Well, this one is old Bretagne pottery. Blue and orange.'

'And?'

'Well, it's nice.'

'A girl thing.'

We found we needed a mattock and made another trip to the garden centre down the hill.

As our efforts began to show in the garden we started to think big. This is fraught with danger.

'How about we make a garden bed.'

'Ok.'

Naturally a garden bed needs a border. We decided to dig up the slates along the washing line and dig them in the ground for a border. One or two red wines and nothing looks too hard. The next day we began bright and early. Those slates were bloody enormous. Some were as big as our aeroplane cabin allowance. They were sunk into the earth by someone with a sadistic bent, and came out one wiggle and jiggle at a time. We then had to sink them into the ground in a different location. It all felt a bit too hard, but when you start something like this, well, we stuck at it knowing our endeavours would be worth it.

So far we had bought a couple of handles and a sieve, but Boomie was hankering for something more. Something with an engine so we went in search of a *tondeuse* (lawnmower). Without a car our shopping was confined to the village, but a quick scout on the internet and we found the prices to compare. Luckily our local garden centre was around the same price. Line trimmers were a different story. We needed to go further afield.

The next big town of St Brieuc has one of just

about everything. We asked Myriam if she was going that way by any chance and made a date.

Landing at Leroy Merlin, which has several of everything and some things that aren't even covered by 'everything' was just what we needed. We had been missing our hardware fix and this cheered us right up.

We looked at combustion heaters, kitchen units, marvelled at the price of a jigsaw compared to Australia and studied bathroom fixtures. I went to light fittings for a good laugh and he went to paint. We met at plywood and decided we should head over the road to the huge garden centre.

The centre had tools and ornaments and poisons and just about everything. What we saw in the way of garden furniture and ornaments only convinced us the French 'style' is one all their own. Pot plant holders covered in glitter with plastic flowers stuck on them didn't float my boat. A concrete goat for the front yard didn't press any of Boomie's buttons.

They also do a line in garden gnomes on Dutch windmills that actually work. And lots of clogs. Those shoes are everywhere.

What we really wanted was the plastic Balinese gazebo with fake bamboo trim. It just nudged the garden gnome with the hubble bubble pipe (that worked) from first place. Some things are just too good to pass up.

There are line trimmers and then there are cheap line trimmers. The old motto of 'poor people pay twice' pricked our consciences and we shelled out for a robust, medium to high range trimmer that wasn't made in China. Ours was German and up to the job. Getting it in Myriam's car for the drive home was the tricky part. It was like packing a giraffe into a shoe box.

We worked in the garden every day and the pile of cuttings and dead things under the plum tree grew to gigantic proportions.

It was while I was surveying our pile of cuttings that we met our back neighbours. They were mightily surprised to see the yard being done and congratulated us on the job. Their yard was immaculate. Their lawn was trimmed, the bushes verdant and their vegetable garden was regimented order. Our garden by comparison was mad woman's breakfast. Marie told me to wait and then came back from her veggie patch with a lettuce. She rolled it down the bank to me in a neighbourly gesture.

'*Merci.*'

I'm not sure, but I think it was a bit of a peace offering you see, when we were cleaning up we found a huge pile of rotting grass cuttings and clippings on our side of the back bank. I think Marie and her husband had been using the Cansot yard as their dumping ground for over 2 years and now we had the job of cleaning it up and getting rid of it. Still, it was a nice thought, and the lettuce was delicious in our egg sandwiches.

The other thing that grew were the blackberries. I like blackberries as a jam, but we had more than our fair share. Every bird within ten kilometres had shat seeds in our yard and we were choking in plants. They are everywhere in France. It's a wonder anyone could invade the country, mired in blackberries as it is.

'C'mon lads, over the top.'

'Hang on, I've got a blackberry bush caught in my trousers.'

Boomie was waging a private war. He went in search of the big guns.

His weapon of choice was Roundup. Not your ordinary garden variety Roundup poison. This was especially designed for *ronce*.

Naturally we needed a pump action pressure bottle for the killing spree. I could see it would be a long and protracted engagement because we'd be going home as summer progressed and once we had left the battle field the blackberries could be on the offensive again.

France is the land of prickles. Not only do they have blackberries, they have, and therefore we have, a bush that has thorns about as big as a dining fork. We also have roses by the bucket load and every one of them has thorns that are designed to catch you every bloody time you walk by or bend down. I was waging my own war with my newly bought secateurs, (which is a French word BTW). Some of the roses had to go. There was one rose that had climbed and clung to the house all the way to the roof line and I cut it back, but grubbing it out was proving difficult so I asked Boomie for help. He put his back into it and with one swing of the mattock he hit rock. I dug down and discovered it wasn't rock, but a path. We started to uncover a concrete path that eventually went right across the back of

Colditz. Pulling the soil away from the wall would alleviate our damp problem.

'This is just like archaeology,' he said.

'Except it hasn't rained,' I replied. I had worked in archaeology for quite a few years and knew a thing or two about digging, usually in the rain.

Because of the lack of rain, we naturally though everyone was just joking when they asked

'Do you like the rain?' This was our second trip to Brittany and we'd only had, maybe, one or two wet days.

In our enthusiasm for gardening we'd bought seeds and now planting them we ironically needed water. We bought a hose.

I will just say right now that the French have no idea about hoses. We bought the best we could find and found it wanting. It is the weakest, knottiest, kinkiest piece of bullshit you are ever likely to buy. It is a nightmare every time we want to use it. It was quickly christened 'the Kinkmaster'. The French might do some things really well, but they don't do hoses. In Australia we have so many to choose from in a variety of anti-kink factors, anti-sun properties and anti-frustration ones that have 5 stars. Boomie and I had been spoilt for choice. We decided that next time we would pack hoses in our suitcases. If we could ship a container load over we'd make a fortune and clean up. The French would marvel at our hoses.

At the end of the day we'd take a tour of our domain with a wine in hand. From our vantage point on the hill we could see miles into the French

154

countryside. The wildflowers were in profusion, the air was fresh and we were happy.

'This was living. This was what it was all about. This is why we came to France.

18

Shopping is a cathartic exercise.

When we had whipped the yard into shape and could see an end to our labours I said I needed more than a second-hand microwave for cooking. The microwave must have heard me because it never worked again.

All the while we waited for OFII to send us something in the post. I went to work with my secateurs to cut the hedge back even further so there was no mistaking our letter box. I still couldn't find our number 50.

Super U did a line in white goods that were cheap and cheerful and there was free delivery, bonus!

First, we needed to make sure our gas bottles were compatible with the fittings on a new stove. Bernadette's stove was ancient as was the gas fitting. It all looked like it would fit and with a wave of our bankcard we purchased a four-burner stove with an oven. It would be delivered on Friday. Although *Super U* had four trucks for delivery standing idle most of the time, Friday was delivery day. I began to dream of the things I could make.

Next we wanted a washing machine. Living on a boat we hadn't had a washing machine to call our own for 11 years. Marinas up and down the coast have laundries at $4.00 a pop. This was getting exciting. Again we were told it would be delivered on Friday. The only problem I could see was that we didn't have a tap with the right fitting under the house or upstairs. The plumber came to the rescue. We were good to go. While we were on a spending spree we bought a microwave. This was one up on Bernadette's, but still only had a dial. The digital age hasn't quite got there on budget microwaves from *Super U*. I felt like all my Christmases were coming at once. What the heck, we bought a fridge too. White goods here were quite cheap. They were of a decent quality, not manufactured in PRC and all had energy ratings that were 4 stars or more. We liked doing business with the French.

The woman at *Super U* informed us that some of our things would need to be ordered so they would come on a Friday…in the future. Starting out with all new stuff was fabulous.

The first to arrive was the stove and for the occasion I decided to roast a chicken. I put the bird on and in about three minutes I could smell gas. Bernadette's hoses on the gas bottle were leaking. We raced to the shop and found the right fittings and came home for a gas repair. All good and I put the chicken on again. In Australia we cook with propane gas. It does the job, but is nothing like butane for heat. I now know the French cook with butane. After about an hour I came inside from the garden to see the house was full of smoke.

'Bloody hell, we're on fire,' I yelled to Boomie

who was out the back. He ran and we raced up the stairs to investigate. The smoke was billowing out the door and I thought we had a major fire on our hands.

'Shit, I know the word for fire Brigade and fire.' I racked my brains as Boomie ventured into the smoke holding his shirt up to his nose.

'*Pompiers. L'incendie,*' I yelled, although knowing the words was as much use as a chocolate teapot in the circumstances.

'It's the chicken,' Boomie said and he turned the oven off. I took a quick look.

My chicken was black. My new sparkling clean stove was burnt with all the spatting fat and the flue at the back had burnt the enamel. Shit. Lesson one; all gasses are not equal.

When the smoke had cleared and I tried to think what we'd have for tea, eggs and veg was a good standby.

I put on the burner to cook a pot of veggies and the flame leapt up at me and nearly took my eyebrows. Lesson two; jets need to be adjusted before you blow yourself up. After reading the instructions in French we ascertained that there are different jets for a better flame application. It's all a learning curve.

Next to arrive was the washing machine. This front loader was basic, but had all the cycles you could want.

We plugged it in and waited. Smart machines are a bit slow. They have computers that need a little think before they actually do something. We waited while it had a bit of a think. Then it filled with water and stopped. Can you imagine two people on their hands and knees under the house looking through the front loader window watching their washing going round – or not as the case may be. The machine took about 80 minutes to do a load. We decided it must be French.

We decided it must be French.

Having a suite of new white goods was a bit surreal. When our fridge arrived, the possibilities were endless. We only had a smallish fridge on the boat and no freezer. Therefore, if we wanted icecream we'd usually go without.

'There needs to be a trial period,' Boomie said.

We went shopping for icecream.

The French love their icecream as much as they love their chocolate. We started on Pistachio, then cherry, chocolate, lime, apple, rum and raisin and

Madagascan vanilla. These things take time to get right. No need to say Boomie loves his icecream. It wasn't like we were getting fat we said to ourselves, because we lived about one kilometre from the shop (each way) and up a hill. It was all the motivation we needed.

We liked to shop every day because that way we can usually get the bargains in the out of date section. It was on one of these expeditions that we met Howard. He lived in a tiny little house, which he explained was 200 years old. He was English and has a wealth of information to impart to us, and he spoke reasonable French. He peppered his conversation with French words and his favourites were,

'*Absolument*,' (absolutely) and '*Exactement*,' (exactly). He's an absolute gentleman albeit with a propensity to talk. It was Howard how told us that our street was named after the local *Comte.* It was Howard who told us that the Roman road at the end of our street was once the only way in and out of the village, and it was Howard who

advised us that the Mairie might be able to help with our OFII.

'*Absolument.*'

Oh and the all-encompassing,

'*Superbe.*'

19

They have Murphy's law in France.

Things were moving along quite nicely, we were getting into the swing of having a two hour lunch, sometimes with wine followed by a nap. This living the French life suited us. We thought we had made the right decision.

It was one morning when I was hanging out the washing I saw something peculiar on the grass next to the house. I went to investigate, but it wasn't quite clear what the 'thing' could be. It was like a mat on the grass. I bent down and quickly realised it was toilet paper. Pulped toilet paper that had been burped onto the grass.

If you have ever seen the Edvard Munch scream you will know how I felt.

We had heard horror stories about French drains, but had convinced ourselves that because we were on the mains we were in a far superior position. Now our noses were in the air for a different reason.

I called Boomie and he inspected our 'mat'.

'Yep. Its toilet paper.' I fetched a shovel.

What do you do with something that is larger than a bread box and on a closer look has faecal matter in it. I dug a hole and we buried the body in the back yard. That particular bush would probably grow quite well compared to its neighbours.

We tried to convince ourselves that it was just a one off anomaly.

'Pfffh. It is nothing to worry about.'

'*Absolument.*'

'*Exactement.*'

I kept an eye on our little problem and in due course it burped again. The pipe from the toilet disappeared into the ground so we couldn't quite understand how this was happening. I dug a bigger hole this time and we buried the evidence. Soon we would be digging our own long drop toilet and calling it our little piece of Australia. It was after a particularly bad (a bit of an understatement) burp that we decided we needed help. Obviously we had a blockage somewhere underground. The inspection port in the pipe on the outside wall was absolutely clear.

We had already had dealings with the plumber and so I nipped over to Fabien and asked if she could ring the plumber for me. He would come tomorrow.

In the meantime we just kept digging holes in the garden. It didn't happen when we flushed, in fact it was quite haphazard and none of it had logic attached to it.

'I wonder if it is even ours?' I mused.

'Shit doesn't travel uphill,' Boomie said.

The plumber was a strapping young bloke. He spoke no English, but a drain is a drain in any language when it's blocked. We showed him our little problem. When you can't speak the language hand signals and a few noises must suffice.

'Bhhhlllllluuuuuuugggggggh.' I tried to mimic a pipe burping.

He bent down and looked at the pipe disappearing into the ground and his knees went into the sodden soil. I knew what had been in that soil.

I wouldn't be a plumber for quids.

We left him to it for a bit. No-one likes to have someone hovering over their shoulder the whole time. When a decent time had passed we went around the back to see what was happening and he had taken our shovel and uncovered not one drain, but two. Something we didn't know we had.

Our house had a crazy system whereby the waste water and the toilet pipe don't go straight into a waste pipe underground but their contents end up in a little sump first. This is covered by a large concrete slab or capping stone. So the contents of our toilet come down the pipe into a sump – open to the elements except for a lid and then when this sump is full they cascade down a pipe hopefully never to be seen again or hit fresh air. The shower and hand basin sump drains into the toilet sump. It all had the look of Louis Cansot to it. It was only later that we saw the very same sumps in the hardware store. I guess if you lose your wedding ring in the drain you always have the idea you can retrieve it before it goes to sump number two with number twos in it.

Our second sump was full. And all this time we were pooing with impunity. Where we went wrong was assuming the drainage system was under some regulation that required the owner of the said poo never to see it again.

The plumber –in short sleeves and NO gloves- (they breed 'em tough in Brittany) then fiddled with our pipes and decided he needed mechanical help. He mimed he was going for the big guns.

Now in Australia when you have a blockage you either get more roughage in your diet or go for an electric eel. These marvels are terrific at whizzing down a drainpipe and chewing up roots and the like. I had seen eels in action many a time as my kids put things down the loo that shouldn't be there. They make short work of a teddy bear, so out blockage should be easy. They are *de rigueur* if you want the job done. We assumed he was going for an electric eel.

While he was gone we inspected our newly found drains. What else might we find?

Our man came back in due course and produced the 'high tech' machine. He had a water blaster with a 50 metre wand. Boomie sucked on his teeth and wondered if it was up to the job.

I mimed an electric eel. Not an easy thing to do let me tell you. I drew a picture, again not an easy task. The plumber smiled and asked for a hose.

Our kinkmaster hose immediately went into spasms at the thought of doing any work. It twisted and knotted itself into something like a macramé hanging pot holder. Even the French plumber wasn't impresses. We laid it out and tried again and the end popped off landing in the sump – number two sump of course and the resultant splash wasn't very nice.

Unperturbed our man reassembled the hose and his water blaster finally was working. To be fair his wand did have a tiny high pressure hole that could probably cut through small worms or filigree roots, but we had a major problem. He stuck the wand down our pipe and we all waited as the build-up of filthy water began to resemble a swimming pool. Then the plumber asked me to go inside and flush the toilet. What he hoped to achieve I didn't know but I did as I was told. After I flushed I opened the window to see where the water would go and as we all watched two dirty great big turds popped out of the sump drain and floated to the top. All think of to say was,

'*Oh, Pardon,*' as I hung out the window. How mortifying. To see your turds in company isn't my idea of participating in the French way of life.

The moment passed, (a bad choice of words) and the plumber resumed his labours. Whatever he was charging he was worth it.

The wand kept on going in and the water coming out when there was an almighty burp and what came out was more than my stomach could handle. I quickly shut the window and retreated inside for a cup of tea.

'Coward,' Boomie said.

'*Exactement.*'

I asked the plumber if he charged by the hour.

'*Oui.*'

Because his attempts weren't working he decided to come from the other direction. We all trooped to the street and watched as he lifted the manhole cover and I got my first look at a French village sewage system.

OH, Pardon!

The pipe outlet was under a second cover which had to be hauled up with a bit of wire and under that was the streets drains. They looked in remarkably good order. We all had a look at our outlet about a metre and a half down the hole.

The idea was to get the blaster wand down that hole and shove hoping to dislodge whatever was blocking us from using the commune's facilities. I took charge of the kinkmaster hose, Boomie was in charge of the waterblaster machine and our plumber was on his belly feeding the wand into the hole.

166

Nothing was happening and so I went to look at the sump for any fall in the level of water.

I gave a shout of joy as all the water whooshed away and I ran down to the boys to tell them the news.

'*Bon.*'

All fixed and it was still daylight hours. Our man packed up his tools and we congratulated him on a job well done. I wasn't going to shake his hand or give him a kiss, although I felt like it. We could now use our drains with gay abandon. We politely asked about the bill and he waved away the notion like we had asked for his first born for a sacrifice. Apparently it just happens later.

We were cool with later.

'The first thing we are going to do is get rid of this sump nonsense.' Boomie had spoken.

'*Exactement.*'

Of course saying it and doing it are two different things. Once our drainage returned to normal we sidestepped the issue of the sumps and just put it on the 'to do' list for later. What we did do was scenarialize on how we would clean up if we had an electric eel. The French would be amazed at our drain prowess. Imagine bringing a container load of eels over and selling them to every plumber. We'd clean up. Make a fortune. It was a wild idea. I'd stick in some brooms while I was at it.

As our plumbing was sorted we decided a trip to the coast was in order. Everyone needs rest and relaxation. The day was warm and we did all the tourist things, only to find on our return that now the drain under the house had burped and all the toilet paper was over ground. It wasn't a welcome sight to come back to after a splendid day by the sea.

'How the hell does our toilet paper end up in the grey water drain?' Boomie asked. It was a worry. Naturally the grey water drain had a sump, but this one was a corker. It was about 600 mm deep and the pipe to empty it was right at the top. What genius would put the outlet at the top of the sump? Unlike Australia where there is an expert for everything, France has a more liberal attitude to home renovations. Everyone can have a go at plumbing. Methinks Louis might have had a hand in the design and execution stages of our drains. That's French engineering for you. It meant that everything from the sink just sat in the drain until you had 600mm of washing up water then it would cascade into the pipe. Now our toilet water was cascading back. It was a hideous thought, as well as a rather bad look.

I collected the shovel and we buried the bodies in the back yard...again. This all happened on Saturday afternoon and there would be no hope of the plumber coming on a weekend. This was rural France after all.

So the only solution to our problem was to bucket it and chuck it. As luck would have it the land next to us was a small plot of meadow. No-one came to look at it, mow it or own it, so now we used it to deposit our deposits. If nothing else happened it would be the greenest meadow in the street.

Cleaning up after yourself isn't the nicest of jobs. It requires a certain amount of dexterity and careful execution. 600mm of sump is a long way down. Boomie devised a scoop from a can and a length of wood and this worked quite well. We'd take it in turns scooping and chucking and putting the hose down the pipe for the flushing in the hope of getting most of our deposits. Naturally when it was my turn to shove the hose down like performing an enema the brass squirter came off in the pipe. Now we not only had a blockage, we had a squirter bunging up the works.

It was while doing this on the Sunday morning, in full view of the road that our neighbour Francis and his crazy dog came by.

It is lucky we don't speak French. We didn't want to explain that our toilet was now back draining into our sump, it would be too embarrassing, so I mimed a blockage as best I could and Francis decided he would take a look. He took his crazy dog home and came back for a better look at the problem. Drainage issues are universal. He bent down like a proctologist on a field trip. Lucky for us we had cleaned the drain and all he saw was a bit of dirty water.

It seems that seeing three people bending over a drain is an invitation. Jacques from across the road came over. He bent down and I could see right away he was an expert with his plumber' crack. He had his trackie pants on and slippers, but that didn't stop him. Francis and Jacques pondered the problem and then Jacques went for tools. He met Marcel in the road who was coming back from the Boulangerie with a baguette under his arm. He also came in to take a look.

There was more conversing about our blockage

and a hose was suggested. Francis took charge and shoved our kinkmaster down the pipe and asked Boomie to turn it on. What can you do when your neighbours are just trying to be nice and helpful? Jacques came back at this point just in time to see one of my turds pop its head out and float to the surface in the sump. Where is a rock when you want to crawl away? Horrified isn't a strong enough word. Again, I was mortified. What can you do? It was there staring up at us. I tried to pretend it wasn't there. Boomie tried not to look at me otherwise he would start laughing. He screwed up his face and then looked away. Oh well,

'just three more Frenchmen who have seen my Australian turd'.

Jacques had fetched a carbon fibre rod that screwed together. No-one has this sort of tool for the 'just in case' scenario. It was obvious that he had drain issues too. In fact, as the men looked on no-one had a look of surprise. It was clear to me that this sort of thing happened all the time. A drain is égout, and *gout* is to taste. Only the French language could have the two words so close together in pronunciation. I wasn't even going there with my rudimentary French!

Jacques got to work and screwed the lengths together, and as my turd had sunk out of sight, he began to feed the rod down the drain. Marcel and Frances encouraged him with a running commentary. He poked and prodded and the rod came up against something hard. All the men looked on.

Then Francis thought he would have a go. He pulled the rod out and started again, with the same outcome. Marcel, a man with a fresh baguette to eat within the next 20 minutes or it would be like a rock, said his goodbyes and left.

Francis stood up and shrugged his shoulders. I wondered if I should offer him soap and a towel, but he was unperturbed by the cholera issue and waved goodbye. We offered to clean Jacques rods for him, but he said it wasn't necessary and just packed up and left. That was enough work, because it was Sunday after all.

And we were still left with a drain that didn't work. What we had all worked out was that the toilet pipe was still blocked and now was slowly filling the Y junction and we had reached the limit.

The only solution was abstinence.

You can only dig so many holes in the garden before the neighbours will start to wonder. Our village has, to our great fortune a decent public toilet. They may be right down the hill, but they work.

'*Superbe.*'

We were used to walking to go to the loo as in Marinas one sometimes has to hike quite a way before relief.

'It's just like being on the boat,' I said.

'*Absolument.*'

We made the public loo our own and left our pink toilet paper in there. The other thing we did was compose a letter via google translate and leave it in the plumber's letter box so he would see it first thing Monday morning. We needed help.

Monday came and went and the plumber didn't come. I thought I had made it clear that it was an emergency.

'We have toilet water coming under the house!!'

Perhaps he was afraid we would not pay the bill? Perhaps we had insulted him? Perhaps google translate isn't all it's cracked up to be?

Meanwhile, Boomie had, what we knew to be

'pink eye' developing. We only knew it to be 'pink eye' because we had watched a movie once where the occupants of an all-male house had the same affliction because they had been farting on each other's pillows. I hadn't been farting, but Boomie had inadvertently splashed himself in the eye with 'dirty' water. The result was a blistering infection that needed codine. I was just about ready to airlift him out, only for the thought that the hospital would have toilets that flushed. It was a close run, but he started to recover. Making the toilet walk when you don't quite feel like it is a test of strength.

'Bloody French and their bloody drains.'

'*Exactement.*'

On the Wednesday when the plumber still hadn't arrived we kinda knew he wasn't coming and to be honest we didn't want to spend more money, so it was a bit of a stand-off. .

Our trips to the loo were co-ordinated with the library and the shops. Bowels can get used to a regular habit and ours were no different.

Our morning trip to the toilet was chilly and the neighbours must have thought we were fitness fanatics, walking at all hours, rain or shine. We could well imagine them exclaiming how those new people just love walking.

'Those two Australian crazy people going for

another walk'. We could be going to the Boulangerie. The French would understand traipsing around for bread. It was the 9.30pm trek that was harder to explain. If only I could have slung a camera around my neck to look like I was going somewhere instead of hiding toilet paper in my jeans pocket.

The up side, and there is always an up-side was that we were getting fit and,

the family that poo together, stay together.

Our drains would need to wait for our next visit.

20

Being French requires a paradigm shift.

Because our drains were under control, or at least not spilling their guts and we still hadn't heard anything from OFII we decided to take a day out of our renovation schedule and go for a bicycle ride to the next village. It was only 6 kilometres or so and the day promised to be clear and warm. Perfect.

We set off on our folding bikes and it felt like a blessed release from all the house troubles. Cycling is a bit of a cathartic exercise. As I peddled my stress level began to drop and things weren't so bad after all. We had packed a small cut lunch for our destination and I could just see us sitting under a tree in the shade, wine, sandwiches and wildflowers. It is one of those quintessential images of France.

We had started off with sunshine, but in Brittany the weather can change in an instant. We had just reached the first little village on our itinerary when the clouds came in and the sun disappeared. This village was having a bicycle race. There was bunting across the road and inadvertently we had cycled into the beginning or end of the race. I expected the peloton to catch us any second. We waved to the crowd of 5 people and they cheered us on. I held up our bottle of wine and the crowd went wild…sort

174

of. At the end of the village a woman called us over and snipped off a flower for me. How nice are the French. We cycled on and about ten minutes later were passed by the peloton all waving and having a jolly time.

The French countryside in Brittany is mainly farming and the place is practically poker-dotted with old farm houses, ruins, barns and we saw a couple of donkeys. There is something to see around every bend. On our journey we came across an old church in ruins, covered in ivy at the crossroads, then further on a huge stone cross marked the boundary of the churches historic domain. We crossed rambling brooks and poplars planted by the side of the road in lines as straight as a Roman road.

The small village we were heading for had a historic listed 11th century church. It dominated the village and you must admire the men who built it all those hundreds of years ago. We found a sheltered spot in the sun and out of the wind and had our picnic within spitting distance of the church and all its history.

After a day like that, working on the house wasn't a priority. We could see heaps of things that needed to be done, but convinced ourselves that without the OFII 'OK' then everything was a bit premature.

Our visit was rapidly coming to an end and we'd be returning to Australia Being in our own house we had slipped into French life and knew we wanted to stay. I knew the French were tardy when it came to paperwork, but we had been patiently waiting for ages for OFII. I went over to Myriam's to seek advice.

'It's France. Don't worry,' she said.

I began to worry.

I went over all the things that we were supposed to do and made sure we had done them. All our boxes were ticked. Then I went on the internet and made sure my list of requirements given to me by the Sydney consulate was the same as the OFII web site.

If you have ever gone cold with dread and just about shat yourself you will know how I felt when I saw the OFII web site.

'Fuuuuuuuuuuckckckckckckckck.'

The Sydney consulate had given us the wrong address. We had sent all our documents to somewhere, but not to the OFII in Rennes. The OFII in Rennes had a completely different location on their web page.

'Holy crap Batman!'

This was really serious. If we didn't get the interview within our time limit then we would need to start the process all over again. The web page was clear on this. That meant that we would need to go to Sydney …again.

'Fuuuuuuuuuuuuuckckckckckck.'

Howard had said that the woman in the Mairie was quite helpful when he wanted things done. I ran down to the Mairie and in my best French tried to explain what had happened.

'Could she possibly see if this new address was the right one and talk to them on my behalf?'

The woman looked up the telephone number and gave them a quick call.

'*Oui.*' This was the right address.

There was only one thing to do. I went to see Myriam.

Once I explained the whole situation…everyone knows the word 'fucked', Myriam said she would ring for us.

Surely, the woman on the phone would see the complete balls up and give us a chance to jump the queue. We had plane tickets to go back to Australia and to lose these as well as our chance to get a residency permit was beyond financially painful. I'm not sure I could stand the strain of selling our house before we had a chance to live in it. I had budgeted everything and staying on for our interview, andchanging our tickets didn't enter into the equation. Never mind we had no-one to look after the boat for an extended period.

After all the blowhard bluster like,

'I'm going to send a complaint the consulate. A blistering email and a letter.' And

'I'm going to complain to the ambassador,' we came back down to earth and realised we needed to negotiate with the OFII.

Negotiating with a French public service entity is a lesson in patience. Myriam rang the number on the web page. She got a recording and was disconnected. She tried again. This time the recording gave her a choice. The public service is the same the world over in this respect. She pressed one and waited. I think we must have been about 125th in the queue. We waited some more and then finally a woman came on the line. Now I don't know much French, but I can just tell when someone doesn't get it. The woman at the OFII couldn't understand why we just couldn't ring ourselves. Why did Myriam need to do it for us? Again, Myriam explained we didn't speak French…unthinkable!

Our whole situation was explained and the OFII officer finally grasped the urgency. What we needed to do was resubmit by post…by 4 o'clock.

It's alright to say by 4 o'clock when you are sitting in an office and have all the necessary printers, scanners and photocopiers at your disposal. I looked at my watch.

It was bloody 11.45. The post office would be closing for lunch in 15 minutes and this being a Wednesday it wasn't reopening.

'Sweet Jesus, not again.' This felt like déjà vu, (a French expression for 'this feels so f*&%ing familiar.)

I had copies of our passports, but I needed more copies of the other documents. Myriam's antique printer was broken so we raced down to *Super U* and photocopied everything then cycled back, (up the hill) to pick up the letter Myriam had written explaining everything, then scooted, with one friggin' minute to spare, into the post office. The woman in the post office assured us the letter would arrive the next day, but we paid for tracking. I'm not suspicious, but…

Myriam met us outside the post and there were a few high fives all round.

Now we just had to wait for our letter of receipt to say we were in the system and on the list for an interview in the future. That is, if OFII were on the same page. With the French you never quite know.

'Don't worry. Come for dinner,' Myriam said.

It was a welcome offer. It beats tearing your hair out and biting your nails to the quick.

When we went next door Myriam's boys were home as well as her mother and it was all go in the kitchen. We were going to have galettes. There is an art to making these buckwheat pancakes that are as big as a hub cap and as thin as a sheet of paper. I took a lesson in cooking as I watched Myriam and her expert wrist action. The first one off the iron was for me and I had it with ham and egg and cheese. They are loaded up with the filling while on the iron and then folded into a quarter. It was absolutely delicious. When we all had a galette grandma brought out some homemade port. It was a heady brew and as we drank and ate and began to relax French was the main language spoken with google translate a competing second.

Grandma's port wasn't the only thing she made and she was trying to explain her other pickling adventures. She grabbed my dictionary and then said she puts

'Testicles,' in a jar.

'Are you sure?'

'*Oui.*' She pointed to the word in my French/ English dictionary. 'Nuts'.

The lads at the table were in hysterics at Grandma's *faux pas*.

Our pronunciation of French lets us down every

time. Someone told us,

'You take the last consonant and throw it in the sea.' This we had discovered as we tried to get our tongues around some of the words. Some words are quite close to the English with Latin origins, others may look the same, but have a completely different meaning. What is working with the language is that people are patient with us. They know we are trying and that is good enough for them.

Galettes also come in a sweet variety. Myriam pulled out all the stops and we had sweet with chocolate and cream. What a perfect end to a perfectly horrible day.

'If we need to go to Rennes, we will go to Rennes.' Myriam said as we raised our glasses in celebration of friendship and testicles in a jar.

'*A la vôtre!*' (cheers)

21

We ache to make new memories.

We were on a countdown as our date to leave came ever closer and we would be going back to Australia. We held our breath that the OFII would get their act together.

All our efforts around the house had been rewarded and now we could stroll around the garden and make plans on what would be the next step. Although it would all need to wait for our next visit. The house had been almost gutted and then made our home with our new appliances and personal touches. It looked like the dream really would come true. And we had walked the village from one end to the other and found a small piece of rural France that we could call home.

On one of these evening strolls through the village we could hear music. Not the head banging variety, but traditional Breton music. We followed the trail and found a municipal building with the windows and doors thrown open to the evening air and about 30 young kids practicing traditional dancing accompanied by a bagpipe looking thing and two reed wind instruments. Some of the children were in traditional aprons and Breton bonnets and clogs, others had pantaloon, (trousers). This was keeping the traditions going strong. We watched for about half an hour and then crept away. Our little village was alive and well if young people were still interested in inheriting the old traditions.

One thing we had inherited was wood worms. These little creatures busily work away eating your furniture until there is nothing left. They aren't as veracious as termites in the breeding stakes, but they are just as hungry.

In the kitchen we had an old oak dresser which was riddled with little pin prick holes. A sure sign of wood worm. Many people have an idea on how to get rid of things. The boat had taught us that! The solution to stop these critters from denuding the house of furniture was chemicals. Very powerful chemicals. *Super U* had such a chemical …Zythothene, a nuclear weapon when it comes to total annihilation.

'They wouldn't sell it at a *Super U* if it was lethal to humans. Would they?'

'*Oui.*' It seems so.

We also purchased masks of the paper variety.

Spraying a toxic chemical in a cupboard is small bickies. We decided while we were at it to do the floorboards from under the house. This would be the apocalypse we needed. After we felt we had ingested enough Zylothene to give our lungs a good work out, we left the house. Over the next few days the worms came out gasping for air and died. Little fat maggoty things with a black dot for a head. The body count mounted. It took the Ashwins more

182

than a week to recover. We added it to the list of chemicals we had survived. Two pack paint with isocyanates, epoxy resin, spray gun cleaner, not forgetting the paint with VOCs. The Ashwins were practically invincible.

'We laugh in the face of chemical warfare. HA!'

Besides waiting for the OFII we were waiting for our lawn-mower. We had pointed to the one we wanted at the local garden centre and the girl said they needed to order it.

'Couldn't we just take this one,' I asked.

'*No.*'

So we waited. She wrote our order in the book and I made mention that we wanted it delivered. I felt convinced that all was according to plan.

Boomie was itching to get stuck into the grass. I wondered if we could borrow the sheep from the house in the village. Grass cutting and manure at the same time.

'The Ashwins have their own manure,' Boomie reminded me. Not that I needed reminding.

So we visited the shop and tried to find out what the delay was all about.

'It is coming.' The French have such an expectant tone of voice when they say, 'It is coming.' We nodded and smiled.

Our leaving date was getting perilously close and we still didn't have our acceptance letter from the OFII or our lawnmower.

We tried one more time at the garden centre. This time I went armed with google translate.

It turned out that our order had been forgotten.

How? I saw her write it in the book. The only solution was to give us the one on the showroom floor.

We could have had it about two weeks ago and Boomie could have been mowing. There was a flurry of apologies and then we just walked the mower home.

The French think we are a little crazy. We don't have a car and we just walk everywhere…all the time…with rubbish, lawnmowers, shopping and to the public conveniences.

Next I wanted to tackle the OFII. This was getting ridiculous. We needed an outcome.

'This is France.' Myriam felt this simple statement summed up the French and their public service, their drains, their bread and the three Breton kiss.

I began to narrow my eyes and so she offered to ring.

I assembled my documents for the battle ahead. I had visa numbers, passport numbers, telephone numbers and everything in-between. Bring it on!

I sat down with Myriam at her computer and she called just after opening time. We were in a queue.

Then a woman answered and Myriam began to explain that she was calling for her Australian neighbours and…the whole story came out again about the address, the documents re submitted etc.

The woman pondered all this and then said.

'*D'accord.*'(OK.)

So with that one little word all our immediate visa troubles would be over. She would send our 'receipt of document' letter to Myriam's email address and all we needed to do was print it out.

I gave Myriam a high five and then realised her printer wasn't working. Not a problem. She could email the letters to me and I'd do it once back in Australia.

'*No.*'

We must keep the letter with us to show that we are legally allowed to stay in the country.

'Why does everything need to be so hard?' Boomie asked.

'What about Howard?'

I was about to advise Myriam we had a solution when she said she'd ask Fabien at the Carrosserie.

I love the internet. Myriam emailed Fabien and Fabien printed our letters and put them in a folder for us. Problem solved. What a team effort.

Now with our *demande d'attestation* in our hot little hands we were on the treadmill for the next step. Except the next step with the interview and the medical to obtain our *visa de long sejour* would need to wait until our next trip. Our boat was languishing in Port Douglas, and we had more than a few loose ends to tie up before we could move permanently to France. And we didn't want to burn all our bridges before we had our visa completely sorted.

'Imagine if we couldn't stay,' I said.

'And we didn't have a boat.'

'We'd be homeless old people,' because there was no way we could afford to re-enter the Australian housing market. I had read on an internet site that Australia was almost top of the list in the world for house prices.

Myriam insisted she take us in the car to the bus stop, which was just down the hill. We waited for the 6.30am bus to take us to St Brieuc and the TGV. In just a couple of months we had made firm friends, made a house into a home albeit without floor coverings or drains, but it was ours and that would colour all our decisions into the future.

With the three Breton kisses we said goodbye to Myriam, I shed a tear (can't help it, I'm built that way) and we waved goodbye. The hour trip to the train and then the three hour train journey would be just long enough to get over my farewell sadness and start planning for our next trip. Having an overnight stop in Paris before we flew to Australia kinda helped too, (I'm only human!).

I had booked an Airbnb near Montparnasse railway station and so we put our bags in the lockers at the station and walked to our accommodation. The tincy wincy little problem was that our internet and call credit on the smart phone had run out the day before and the apartment had a code to get in the door. We couldn't ring or text. We waited outside the door in the rain hoping for someone to come by. And they did, but once inside the courtyard we were confronted with another code lock. These Parisians can't be too careful.

I needed to ring our host, but without a phone that worked…well have you ever tried to find a public phone that worked in a big city and then

186

discovered you need a credit card arrangement and the nearest tabac shop is probably in Aleppo.

We knew the French were about the nicest people we had met and so I asked the street sweeper if he had a phone. Everyone these days has a phone, it's a given.

He was the sweetest man. He phoned for me, and translated for me and wrote the codes down for me.

With the means to get into the building we found our host and her wonderful Parisian flat.

Somehow, we didn't quite feel like tourists in Paris. We felt we had crossed that threshold and were part of the big picture of France.

Sitting at an outdoor café, drinking beer and watching the world go by Boomie said,

'I think we have found our little bit of paradise.'

We just hoped the OFII wanted us to stay in paradise as much as we did.

'Absolument.'

Coming home.

22

Home is where the heart is…

Leaving France and arriving in Australia can all be accomplished in one sentence. In reality it is a back breaking exercise that takes all your stamina and a few osteo paracetamols. I had bought a few bottles of red for friends and packed all but one in my suitcase. The spare went in my backpack and I then donated it to French customs because I stupidly forgot that airplane travel these days is fraught with danger. We boarded out flight and promised France that we would return. We would have one foot in each hemisphere for a while yet.

Arriving in Cairns to endless sunshine felt very familiar. It wasn't long before we slipped into our usual routines and wondered if we had ever been to France. We had some big decisions to make regarding our finances and how we hoped to keep all the balls in the air.

The first thing was, as Boomie succinctly put it,

'To stop the bleed.' This meant leaving the marina and anchoring for free. We had anchored many times for free, it just takes a bit of logistical figuring out. The next thing to do was start saving like crazy.

The months ticked by and we knew a Port Douglas summer was on its way. This is a ghastly time of the year when the humidity is about 90% and the heat is fierce.

'We need to go back for our visas,' I said.

'We should really get our drains sorted and we wanted to cement under the house,' he said.

'We could be cold instead of hot.'

This last one was the clincher. We could have a cold Christmas, maybe snow. Boomie had never had a white Christmas.

Booking our tickets made the whole thing a reality. We'd be arriving in December and be staying for the whole winter. Our first cold season in donkey's years. On paper we looked like we belonged with the jet set. We had been overseas twice in one year and a quick trip to Sydney.

The first thing I did was pack the front door key, the only one. We had tried to get another cut in Mossman North Queensland, but they couldn't find a blank that even came close.

The next thing I did was take up knitting. I hadn't knitted in years and now it all came back, just like riding a bicycle.

We had lived in the tropics for about 20 years and you need a cardigan or sweater like a bald man needs a comb. Boomie needed beanies and scarves. I needed scarves and berets (it's France after all).

We went shopping for wool and I went to work. Although it was 'winter' in Port Douglas it was still warm. I borrowed a friend's boat with aircon so I could knit in comfort. I could have a 1.5 metre scarf on my lap and not sweat.

We also needed woollens.

The tropics have a winter that lasts 'bout a week. For that week all the shops bring out their woollens and hope for the best. Then around the beginning of September they start selling them off…cheap.

Never one to miss a bargain we started to trawl the shops.

One never quite knows how cold, cold really is, when the most I had worn was a thin cotton cardigan about four years ago in a vicious cold snap that made the thermometer drop to 20 degrees Celsius.

Luckily the shops had heaps of jumpers/ pullovers/sweaters. We hadn't really bought anything for ourselves for years so this was all new and exciting. We had survived on shorts and t-shirts and sandals. I had a dress or two so I could feel like a girl now and again, but we just didn't splash out on things.

We started stockpiling in our suitcases, getting quite carried away because we could get pure new wool for 60% off. Then we saw jeans for ridiculously low prices. Boomie said that if they fit, I should buy two. I can't argue with that logic. Australia has cheap clothing because a lot of the stuff is made in China. It has a life and you only get what you pay for, but if you are prepared for the inevitable then it is a bargain. In France the clothes are a bit more up market with a price to match. A great many of their clothes are made in France. The Ashwins went for cheap and cheerful.

Our suitcases were beginning to fill, when

Boomie said we should make a killing on sheet sets and quilt covers in the stocktake sales. We bought several and then I saw flannelette sheets. These are just about the cosiest things on the planet. We had to have them at 50% off.

'Do we need pyjamas?'

We had been sleeping sans nightwear for well over 20 years, but it was just the thought of having winter jimjams that found us buying a pair of men's check PJs each at around $7.00. PJs need slippers. We found some out on sale for $3.00. Somehow we had to fit it all in our suitcases.

Then I casually mentioned that Bernadette's frying pan was a pain in the neck. It was aluminium and designed so that everything either burnt or got stuck.

We went in search of cookware. Now I had to fit a non-stick frying pan and a non-stick wok in my suitcase. The airport x-ray machine would see two discs and think BOMB!

When you see 40% off underwear and socks it's a given they would need to fit in the case too.

'This is getting ridiculous,' Boomie said. He tried to fit his new woollen coat in his case.

'We need to stop,' I said while putting 100 tea bags into zip lock bags for the trip.

'We can't possibly take all this stuff.'

So we called in our faithful removalists and with a wave of our credit card they would pack our stuff. We sent our tools and homewares. With tools we could really get started on things.

A closing down sale is always a chance for last minute shopping. Boomie wanted a chainsaw.

I saw light fittings that were more to my taste. We found gardening gloves at low prices and kitchen tiles by the box that ended up being around 29 cents each. All this we sent home. I was an old hand at the inventory in French and the bonus would be that we'd be home when everything arrived in early January.

And then, out of the blue we received a letter from the Notaire. I couldn't imagine what he would want with us at this stage. I opened the letter and found a cheque. Somewhere along the line I had paid part of his bill twice. At the time I remember thinking that I'd actually paid, but I trusted him to know what he was doing and left it at that. Now, he was refunding our money, or some of it anyway. It was nice to know the French were honest.

We knew we would be going back to our drain problem and thinking realistically who wants to traipse down to the public toilet in the cold. We needed to get them seen to before we arrived. The trick was to get the plumber interested. Perhaps Myriam might have better luck.

I emailed her with our problem. The good thing about gmail is that they have a little button that lets you choose -translate this page.

I constructed a letter using simple language and she said she would see what she could do.

True to her word she replied.

Goodnight Lovers

I went Plombier to the problem of drainage of pee and poo .... and it will go see

He seemed to say that there has roots in the pipes and he is afraid that this remains butcher constantly.

He wonders if he will have to fart to remove the roots ... but in any case, it will pass.

 I await his estimate
Here, it's getting a little chilly in the morning and evening. By day, it's still the sun.
But a good glass of wine will warm us the autumn and winter evenings.

Hope to see you soon ....

I knew the plumber was good, but farting to remove the roots…that's a classic. If all it took was a fart, Boomie and I could have fixed the problem ages ago. My turbo charger kicks in quite regularly. When we were walking up the hill from the shops Boomie often needed to engage his turbo. French cheese and bread is a killer when it comes to wind.
Obviously google translate still has a way to go.

When our removals had been removed and our bags packed it was just a matter of waiting. The trip would be a doddle this time as we knew where to go, and how to get there. I rechecked our train times, our bus tickets and our all-important OFII documentation. Everything was on order.

Every day I looked at the temperature in Brittany. It was slowly dropping as Port Douglas heated up.

23

Getting there is half the fun. The other half is torture.

My mother often said I could sleep on a barbed wire fence. There was little chance of sleeping on the plane although we did nod off now and again and take up mouth breathing like it was a sport. We flew from Cairns and because we left in the evening all our flight was conducted throughout the night. That sounds like heaven, except they want you to eat when in reality it is your 3am. I don't know how to describe the agonies I go through as I think on the price of the ticket and not taking the meal on offer. I like to get my monies worth. We ate everything on offer. Sleeping with a crick in your neck and your neighbour watching non stop kung fu isn't very restful.

I also had fat ankles. I had purchased pressure stocking for the trip, but when I tried them on in the tropics I couldn't get the darn things up. Boomie had a go and he looked very fetching although a wax job wouldn't have gone astray. So I left them to become paint strainers.

We arrived at Charles de Gaul with our eyes hanging out knowing we still had a whole day of travel ahead. Paris (that name always excites me) was -1 degrees. Our tropical bodies took a minute to digest that number and then we dived into our suitcases for woollens. I'm so glad I learned to knit.

And take up mouth breathing like
it was a sport

Suitably kitted out (I just had to wear my beret) we made our way to Montparnasse train station and the first leg of going home.

Montparnasse services the west of the country. It is a bustling station with hot coffee, a blessing, and patisseries to welcome the weary traveller. The whole thing revolves around a big announcement board.

We positioned ourselves and waited, looking at the board for any new announcement regarding our platform.

This is a ritual that everyone adheres to with steadfast dedication. The reason is simple. When you buy your ticket –automatic –automated –and modern – there isn't a platform number on it. Now if it was me, and the same train came in at the same time every day without mishap and the other trains could be relied upon to do the same, I'd assume that the platform would be available. The French don't go as far as assumptions.

So with ticket in hand all eyes are focussed on the big 'click over' board.

The crowds gather, and as your train flicks to the top of the list at the 30-minute mark, knuckles and fingers tighten onto handles, feet shuffle, scarves are tucked in and everyone waits.

At <u>precisely</u> 10 minutes to departure the little black squares flick over to reveal the platform number. And they're off. Old women in furs, mothers with prams, men in thick coats and hundreds of suitcases on wheels scramble for a place on the train. Not that it's that ad hoc. We all have reserved seats – you can't get on the train unless you have one. But 10 minutes to get everyone seated is a bit optimistic.

As people walk down the platform the pace quickens. Everyone just gets faster and faster, then people begin to peel off and it all just works in that very French sort of way.

We lugged our bags on board and settled down to watch our fellow passengers. To pass the time we make up stories about the, histories and try to guess if they have ever been serial killers. A man opposite me was a little strange. He had a satchel full of torn out magazine pages. As he read each one he'd screw it up and put it in the bin. Obviously, a serial killer!

There was no chance of sleeping on the TGV. We didn't want to miss our stop. Our schedule was tight, but we'd done it before and knew if all went according to plan it would work. When the announcement came through that because of technical work, our train would be ¾ hour late. It was a bit of a concern. Our only bus from St Brieuc to our village was at 4:30. We'd still have 40 minutes up our sleeve, but knowing a thing or two about the French way of doing things I thought that was cutting it fine. The French have a scrupulous, almost fanatical German like attitude to timetables – as long as everything is according to plan. Throw a spanner in the works and then they shrug their collective shoulders and roll their eyes. There was quite a bit of eye rolling in the carriage as the occupants made noises of discontent.

The ¾ hour turned into one hour when the train just stopped. There came that time when I was so tired I really didn't care anymore. We'd find a bush to sleep under if we missed the bus. I was running on empty.

The highlight of the trip was watching a man without a ticket get into strife. The conductress summoned another conductor and they tried to find out why he didn't have a ticket. The thought of someone actually not doing the right thing was a mystery.

'But, <u>why</u> don't you have one?'

The other passengers were agog, but trying not to look like they were looking and listening. We watched like spectators at a football match.

The police were summoned at the next stop and they trooped on board and escorted him off. Then to my amazement they shook hands and sent him on his way. We'd read the situation completely wrong or French pragmatism had saved the day.

Our train, once past the 'technical difficulties' went full steam ahead and we ended up only 30 minutes late. Plenty of time to catch our bus. The only obstacle was the public squatter that needed to be used.

'Why didn't you go on the train?'

'I didn't need to then,' I said.

The public toilet is a dark, smelly place. The door to the squatter is almost on the street and people walking by can see your feet, or anything else for that matter. I off loaded my backpack, coat, scarf and gloves and mentally prepared myself. Boomie stood guard as I ventured inside. At nearly 4.30 in the afternoon the sun is setting. Without a light it is a bit hit and miss. Then Boomie thought he'd better take the opportunity. I re-dressed on the street and he undressed and all I can say is I'm glad he was the one to flush. He came out with wet shoes and trouser legs. Welcome to France.

The bus ride to our village was an hour of remembering landmarks, villages and the Brittany countryside. It looked very different in winter. By the time we put our key in the front door it was dark.

Boomie had broken the kitchen light on our last visit so there was no light in that room. Luckily the street light was right outside the window. I also had the torch facility on my mobile phone. They would do in the circumstances.

We threw our bags inside and legged it to *Super U* for food and wine.

I cooked pork sausages and eggs by streetlight

then we put on our new PJs and snuggled down
under our 4★ quilt listening for the village bell and
our new boiler slowly bringing the heat to the house
and breathing life into its bones once again.

24

Life is full of surprises.

When our body clock is out of whack anytime is a good time. I woke up at 1am French time ready to start the day. Boomie wasn't far behind. Bernadette chimed six times and it felt like home. Big ideas often happen when you are talking in the dark. We made plans on what we hoped to achieve on the trip and top of the list was getting OFII sorted.

It turned out our priority was getting the wardrobe open. My winter coats were hanging up in there and the door refused to co-operate. The key was useless. Mr Crowbar came to the rescue and I could access my winter things and our other bedding.

The boiler was behaving itself and slowly the house began to warm up. And as it warmed it started to make noises. Creakings and groans and ticks invaded the quiet.

The list of priorities grew as getting a kitchen light moved to top of the list. We went to *Super U* for a light bulb. With ancient wiring hanging from the ceiling Boomie did a Louis hatchet job and we had success. One naked light bulb might not be the prettiest light in the house, ('cause nothing beats a clog light) but it worked.

The next 'priority' was our drains.

No-one wants to walk down to the village in the early morning when it is still dark and cold. And the public toilets only have those awful stainless-steel bowls without a seat. Not conducive to having a good snap.

'Perhaps, just perhaps the drains have drained away while we were elsewhere.'

'Perhaps the plumber has farted and all's well.' Using your own toilet shouldn't be so stressful.

'What is the most that can happen?'

'It's not like it would be a surprise.'

'We know the dangers now.'

'It's only poo after all.'

'And it's our poo.'

We started using our loo.

I'm not sure about anyone else, but in the dark when you are tired, life can get a bit disoriented. I woke up to Bernadette chiming and jumped out of bed, not really knowing what was going on, and thinking I was still on the boat. I ran straight into the sharp corner of the wardrobe and hit my head. Oh, just brilliant. Just before the all-important medical I would have a lump the size of a boiled egg on my head. My swearing woke Boomie and he fell out of bed tangled in bedding. We decided to have a cup of tea and try again for a good night's sleep.

The house was getting used to us too, and we came to the conclusion it was slowly moving. The doors didn't close like they had, the floor board gaps were widening and it felt a little out of whack. This was confirmed when Boomie found his spirit level and we tested the door frames. We could only think that the heaters were swelling the underfloor beams and they were settling into the warmth after years of cold weather. It reminded me of the nursery rhyme about there was a crooked man who built a crooked house.

'It's been here for 70 years, it's not going to fall down.' Boomie's words were some comfort.

'It's made of stone and bricks.'

To me it was now a living thing. I began to listen for its quirky noises in the night. It was all part of ownership.

On our last visit we had subscribed to the internet via the local library. There WIFI (pronounced wi and in window and fi as in fill), was reliable and cheap. This trip we subscribed for a year. Most of the time the internet was fast and efficient. But the other times it was abysmal. It would drop out, stop and not restart. The librarian, Christine couldn't understand our limited French and would just shrug and smile and reboot. The library had odd opening hours, but we were allowed to use the WiFi 24/7 by standing out in the cold like factory workers on a smoke break. On one of the rare occasions the library was open for two hours we were sitting in the warm and an elderly gentleman walked in with a briefcase. He nodded and we said,

'*Bonjour.*'

'*Bonjour,*' he answered. Christine popped up and began to fawn.

'*Bonjour M' comte.*

There is nothing like hobnobbing with French aristocracy to put a smile into your day. I studied the old man whose family had probably escaped the 'national razor'. –otherwise why would he be here to carry on the bloodline?

He was in his 90s, or so Howard told us, and a very personable man. He looked harmless to me. We lived on the street named after him. We had walked all over his village, seen his large imposing house, followed his wooded and walled grounds around the town and here he was in the library getting on the internet in the computer room. It looked like Christine was teaching him computer basics. Even the aristocracy need a facebook page!

I added it to the list of things I could write home about. In the '70s I had been on television. In the '80s I had met the Queen of England and exchanged words. The '90s saw my first book published. Now, I had bought a house in France, and met a *Comte*. Life was sure interesting…oh, and I had dug up dead people.

Getting accustomed to the winter takes a bit of a shift in what can be achieved with so little sunlight. Whereas we had enjoyed long twilights last time, this time the sun was set by 4:45 and didn't venture over the horizon again until around 8:45.

We found ourselves staying in bed until 9am, an unheard-of occurrence for the Ashwins. We'd always been early risers. Languishing in bed can be quite addictive. It soon became a routine to make coffee and snuggle down waiting for sun to come up. Our days were getting shorter and shorter and some days we didn't get out of the house until 10:30. Then, by the time we had walked to the shops and back, and had a cup of tea it was almost lunch. After lunch a quick nap or a read and then about one hour of work in the house or the garden and the cold began to creep in, the sun began to go down and we'd be thinking of heading inside for a cup of tea and cake. It was a heady mixture of doing practically nothing at all and enjoying it. We had been flogging ourselves on the boat for the last 2 years and it felt like a well-deserved break.

And all the time our toilet was behaving itself.

'I don't know where it's going, as long as it doesn't come back.'

This situation couldn't last. We knew this and so contracted an English-speaking fellow, Mark to come and dig up the pipe.

'It's only got water in it right?'

'Um…'

We explained the situation regarding an electric eel.

'Have you heard of a mole?' he asked.

A mole, Mark said was a machine that had a thumping action. It was relentless in its quest.

'Trouble is, it would,' he said 'thump right through terracotta pipes, plastic pipes and anything that got in its way.' It sounded like a terminator, rather than a cute little mole or an eel.

'Dig 'em up.' Mark's suggestion sounded like a good one.

Christmas was just around the corner and so he said he would start after the holiday. I hoped we could hold out until then.

With an old bit of pipe and some handy, Louis

like, fixings we rigged up a system whereby our shower water and hand basin waste water would go straight onto the grass. This would take the pressure off the toilet pipe, never mind it looked like something struck my lightening.

Next, we took the unanimous decision not to put paper down the toilet. We called it the Greek solution. If you have ever been to Greece you will know what I mean. In Greece the pipes are so narrow they will not take anything other than that which they were designed. All paper goes in a wastepaper basket next to the loo. The Ashwins were turning continental. We just had to hang out until Christmas was over.

Knowing your way around a place is a comforting feeling. We were taking up walking with vim and vigour because our bike brakes were sorely in need of restoration. It's a bit of excitement to the day starting off down the hill with the wind in your hair only to realise the brakes don't work…at all. It was a tense moment before I jumped off and managed to stop. Boomie's round of applause was the icing on the cake.

It looked like something struck by lightening

The first stop was the *la Déchetterie*. In our absence we discovered the dump had had an upgrade. And horrors, they had cleaned out the shipping container. I only managed a cook book by good ol' readers digest and a wooden duck. Not that I needed a wooden duck or only had 2 in a set of 3, but when you see a wooden duck just staring back at you and it looks antique, hand carved and kinda cute, well it's best to have it. There is a saying – Nothing haunts you like the things you didn't buy. So True. I'd been living with a haunting for neigh on 30 years about a particularly nice pair of second-hand gloves I saw in Colchester, England in the 80s. They were leather – fur lines with rabbit and I ached for them and didn't buy them. So the duck came home.

The other thing we discovered in the village was the Catholic second-hand shop. This little shop occupies the ground floor of a very old building just behind the church of 1575. The shop is open only twice a week and then only for an hour or two. Inside the clothes tell a sad story. Everything is very neat and ordered, but all the clothes are from old people. The village is populated, in the main, by dying inhabitants. The little women who operate the shop are chatty, friendly and there was one that knew all about us.

The boat, the house, our circumstances – everything. We wondered how until she said she lived just up and around the corner and knew Myriam. Apparently, our business is everyone's business. All the women then asked questions, talked up a storm and were more than helpful. I found a great red pure wool coat for five Euros. We were given a chocolate to send us on our way, (what else would it be, but chocolate in France). The next day I went back for a hand knitted wool jumper. This time it was two Euro. I love a bargain, and our 'neighbour' gave me the lowdown on the owner of the jumper, the woman who knitted it, where she lived – and died. Such is life in our little village.

The garden had burgeoned in our absence and the hedge out the front was letting the neighbourhood down. Hedges in this part of France are almost a national sport in that they are super competitive when it comes to trimming. Some are nearly 4 metres high, but cut like a hot knife through butter. Others are small and not a leaf out of place. Some are so level on top you can only suppose a theodolite was used. We had something resembling a dreadlocks convention. Thick bits, straggly bit and ragged bits poked out. We also had blackberry woven into the mix.

'We need tools.' Boomie had spoken. We went in search of a hedge trimmer. We'd been eyeing off hedge trimmer in Australia, but decided to buy something that could have a warranty in France.

Neither of us had experience as owners of a hedge. It looks easy enough and the machine makes quick work of the sticking out bits, but it is a bit like cutting your own hair. Tricky to get just right. We set to work to make a rectangle

and as a first attempt it was a decent effort. Boomie waved the magic wand over the hedge and I cleaned up the mess.

The pile of grass and cuttings that we had collected on our last visit was still down the back and now we added to it, by about another metre. It looked like an art instillation with mounds, dead branches and now newly cut green and gold hedge trimming on the crown. The French neighbours thought we were quite peculiar, trimming our hedge in winter, but we are those crazy Australians that walk, so anything is possible. While out walking one afternoon we were discussing the hedges we saw growing on a tall bank.

'How the hell does he cut that?' Boomie pointed to the neat trim on the bank. I looked up and my knitted beret just disappeared. One minute it was there on my head, the next gone. We looked around on the ground, but couldn't see it until Boomie looked up. There on an overhanging blackberry bush was my beret. The blackberries were fighting back.

Tricky to get just right

Boomie was still at war with our blackberries so as we were blessed with a few days of sunshine they all received a dose of roundup. The lawnmower was put to work plus the line trimmer. We'd do just enough to tame the yard, before the cold set in.

Coming from the tropic to a Northern European winter everything is a wonderment.

Our village is in a dip in the countryside. From our vantage point half way up the hill we have a commanding view of rural France, including the wind turbines that dominate the landscape. Because the village cascades down to the Church in the valley we collect fog like others collect stamps. The fog comes across the flat land and then drops into a 'pea souper' around *centre ville.* Some days we couldn't see the carrosserie across the road. It makes walking a little spooky as sounds are muffled and people loom out of no-where. Another thing that took us by surprise is the lack of wind. Boating people need to be attuned to the weather and we are no different. Wind is ever-present up in Far North Queensland.

Trade winds from the South East are a constant reminder of the weather. In our part of France the wind is practically non-existent. We have a line of tall majestic pine trees just east of the house and every day I look for movement. Every day is the same. Nothing. It certainly makes a change.

To remind ourselves how cold it really was, we bought a thermometer and hung it outside the window. We could now report to our family and friends, frying in an Australian summer, how cold it was at any given time of the day. It had a fascination all its own. Things were getting ridiculous when Boomie woke me one night to tell me it was zero degrees.

'To get a true reading it needs to be on the washing line'. So of course, to read the damn thing we put on hats and scarves, and took the mobile phone, with the torch facility, out to the washing line to read the temperature. When you have lived in temperatures of 25 to 30 Celsius for 25 years or more the cold is certainly different. Walking to *Super U* where the temperature is digitally displayed we pride ourselves that we have the same reading.

The other thing we like to do is second guess the temperature. If my eyeballs are hurting, it is usually less than 4 degrees Celsius. If Boomie's moustache had droplets on it the temperature is around 6. It's not a lifelong occupation, but it's fun.

To read the damn thing we put on hats and scarves.

Our walks have a predictable path and I always marvel at some of the houses we have christened 'the fresh air fiends'. Their windows and doors are flung wide open in all temperatures and weathers. If the sun is out the bedding is out too. It is a continental thing to air your quilt on the windowsill. But these people throw the whole house open to the elements. One house has French double doors onto a balcony and every time we walk past they are wide open.

They breed 'em tough in these parts. The Ashwins are snug as bugs in rugs in our house. I have aired the house once or twice on a glorious sunny afternoon, but because we are paying for our heating, it is a quick open and shut affair. Like they say about boating 'a hole in the ocean where you throw your money', it would be just throwing Euros out the window.

214

We are not the only ones that walk. Every Sunday, that day when the village does nothing, there is a parade past the house of men going to the *Boulangerie* first thing in the morning. I think it is a man thing. I have yet to see the female of the species coming home with a baguette under her arm. The French are great walkers and we often see the same faces on our travels. We know the man with the white dog, the woman with the fur hat, the old man with the two hiking stick and the list goes on. They are all very cordial,

'*Bonjour Monsieur et Madame.*'

'*Bonjour.*'

Getting dressed in the morning is a bit different too. In the tropics it is either this t-shirt or that t-shirt and a pair of shorts. Teamed with a pair of sandals and you're done. People don't just realise what it is like to live in a temperature range of 5 degrees. After wearing basically the same thing for years having the choice of jumpers, cardigans, jeans, long sleeve t-shirts etc it was all new and different.

And because we wear woollens we collect slut balls under the bed. They are so prolific I reckon I could knit a jumper before winter ends. Where do they all come from? The other thing that collects are fluff pixies

Don't know what fluff pixies are? Men, and Boomie in particular, have a habit of collecting fluff in their navels. It's always blue and it's there every day. If I saved it I could make a throw rug. The tropics were never like this.

One of the best places to be when it is cold, apart

from under a 4★ quilt is next to the heater. We have old cast iron ones that look like zoo railings. Boomie loves nothing better than to park his derrière on the heater. But you can have too much of a good thing it seems. He had been slowly cooking and when he showed me the results he looked like a grilled steak at a 5★ restaurant. It could be a talking point.

'Have you seen my husband' medium rare?'

'*Absolument.*'

.It was zero degrees and we were out bright and early for a change, when Boomie nearly came a cropper (Aussie slang for a fall). Icy conditions on the footpaths were a new adventure. He skidded to a halt at the Mairie steps and grabbed my hand and we started giggling. Seeing two older Australians gingerly making their way down the main street while the locals walked about with impunity must have been a rare sight. It certainly was fun for us.

I was walking ahead on a narrow footpath when I heard a loud crack and turned around expecting to see Boomie flat on his back, but he was still upright. The source of the noise was blackbirds. They were dropping chestnuts from the flying buttresses on the church to the road to crack them open. The street was littered with shells. It reminded me of the mynah birds in Port Douglas who congregate in the car parks picking insects out of radiator grills on cars.

The wildlife is quite resilient in the cold. The pigeons are puffed up like New York rappers in puffer jackets, the small birds stick to the eves of the houses and the blackbirds hop around on the

216

chimneys keeping warm. Boomie has a soft spot for animals and was feeling sorry for the birds in our back yard. So with a bit of stale baguette on offer I drilled a hole in one piece and threaded a string then set it out for the birds. And there it hung…for days. French birds have the same sensibilities as their human counterparts when it comes to day old bread.

    'Jamais' (never).

So we bought some seed. We knew we had a resident woodpecker and what looked like blue tits, but were hoping for a whole show of native birds. Apparently French birds are discerning eaters. They spurned our seed. What we watched them do with steadfast regularity was flick the leaves over on the ground looking for bugs. I saw a blackbird do a happy dance when he found one and swallowed. The smaller birds hang on to the oak tree and pull off the bark in

a frenzy of destruction looking for morsels. Our woodpecker drills holes in the dirt – quite a few – at last count about 100 and hunts for grubs. He's tenacious, beautiful to watch with his bright red plume, but not too successful.

'*Jamais*' (never).

We had brought over our boat binoculars this time. Every other time we had wished we had them. Now we could watch our feathered friends up close. We watched the weather, the wind turbines, the hills and the neighbours – just pretend I didn't say that!

Our neighbour on the meadow side has a beautiful large stone house. It is well kept, the gardens are professionally done twice a month and no-one lives there. I have watched this house looking for signs of life. We did meet the owner once. He was driving away in his very expensive car and stopped to introduce himself. He leaned out of his car window and offered a hand covered in gold rings, his wrist dripping in Omega watches and gold bracelets. I leaned in expecting to see a gold tooth. Everything about him reeks wealth. He was friendly enough, but there is just something about someone who keeps a perfectly good house, in perfect order and doesn't live in it, or even go inside. It's not spying when you are an author.

218

We have christened him the Gaelic Gangster.
'It's a tax dodge.'
'He's probably on witness protection.'
'It's his parent's property.'
'He's obviously a drug dealer.'
We watch and wait.

Coming over in winter meant that we didn't work too hard, but just enjoyed village life, albeit in the cold.

A much-anticipated event in the village was the annual Christmas Fete. This market was a time for everyone to come out and have a bit of fun, a bite to eat, participate in fancy dress and generally let their hair down. We went along to watch the French let their hair down.

We strolled down to the village square in the chill of the morning and were met with a goat chaperoning a pony ride. Apparently the two animals were inseparable and where nanny goes the pony goes. The children getting a ride in the cart were laughing as the goat butted the man with the holster to get a move on. The manure was collected by women in housecoats, for the veggie garden I presumed. The market stalls were crowded with handmade items. A bloke was weaving big baskets to store logs by the fire, a women had made Christmas decorations out of bits of wood and hand kitting was in abundance.

The French are great *gastromonique* people. They love their food. The galette caravan had a queue and the woman doing the cooking had an expert flick of the wrist through years of practice. The galettes were about 450mm across and she just flipped and tossed and folded them like an art form. We had one each. I went with lemon and sugar, Boomie had his with cream and chocolate. Then we wished we had looked for savoury first before our dessert. The stall next door had a man stirring a big cauldron full of what looked suspiciously like tripe. We saw him pour a whole bottle of white wine into the brew and stir. He smacked his lips and asked if we would like some. I feigned full and we hurried away to the home make cake stall. As the day progressed the fancy dress was judged, the children flogged off biscuits for fundraising and we talked to a wood turner about his fantastic creations. He had bowls and trays and I picked out a tiny little box with a mouse carved on top.

'It is for the teeth of children,' he explained. It was so cute.

'In France the tooth fairy is a mouse.' I like that.

I put it on my mental list to keep an eye out for carved mice at *la déchetterie*.

There was also a surfeit of hedgehog related carvings, knit wear, children's clothing motifs, and toothpick holders. All very French.

The cheese stall was doing a roaring trade in stinky cheese, the stinkier ones were touted as 30 years old. They would probably get to 40 years if they smelt as bad as they looked. The rind was a green/purple colour and had the look as if it had been in the sun too long. It was a wrinkly, shrivelled thing and on the bottom had, to my eye, hair. Not the most appetising of cheeses. We summoned the courage to try some other cheeses on offer and were surprised how good they were. I couldn't go past their fig concoction. It was a big pie shaped slab of pressed dried fig and almond. My slab felt like a kilo of heaven.

Just the thing for *goûter* (This is an afternoon snack around 4pm. It is especially for children because typically the French eat around 7pm or later). The Ashwins partake of *goûter*. Well, we need to start somewhere if we are going to 'immerse' ourselves!

The next stop had to be the wine tent. This was three deep at the bar before 11:30. The locals had no sensibilities about waiting until after lunch. There were a lot of farmers with rubber boots, a Wookie and about a dozen of Snow White's dwarfs all hard at it. Boomie raised his money and our drinks were passed back with

'*Joyeus Noël.*' (Merry Christmas).

A quaffy red went down a treat and we then concluded our rounds with another look at the tripe stand. It was doing great business. I was tempted, but only for a second. Offal isn't my favourite food. After working in an abattoir (French word) and seeing the offal room on a daily basis, I could forgo the innards of a beast without the least bit of guilt, French cuisine or no French cuisine.

'This is what retirement is all about,' I said to Boomie as another day slipped by, my to be read' pile shrank, we roamed the town, and I began to dabble in French cuisine myself.

I had my French cuisine book from *la déchetterie* to whet my appetite. All I needed was butter and cream; gallons of it.

I cooked cakes, *Normandie* apple tarts, French apple biscuits and had a go at galettes with lashings of cheese and ham. We tucked into garlic chicken casserole - *Poulet en cocotte à l'ail*, beef with carrots - *beouf aux carottes,* fillets of duck - *Aiguillet te de canard* and trout with creamed leeks – *truites à la crème dé poireaux.* It was a gastronomic adventure. Just looking at the pictures in my cook book made me want to try everything.

I mentioned to Myriam I was cooking *lapin,* (rabbit).

'Be careful how you say it,' she said. '*La pine,* is slang for the male sex parts.'

I could just see the conversation.

'What are you cooking tonight?'

'*La pine.*'

'One piece each apparently'.

There was a tricky moment when I made an old-fashioned egg custard tart and because of the slight lean of the house all my nutmeg ended up on one side. This was just like cooking on a boat!

The French are great believers in using what is in season. *Super U* make a rather pretty display of what's in season and what's local. I try to be French, sans housecoat, and buy local. The French have really good ingredients and everything tastes as it meant to be. Apples are old varieties and taste like real apples. Chicken has that old Sunday roast flavour of my childhood and when cooked isn't full of water. I was told that hormones are banned in France. I don't know if it is true, but whatever they are doing or not, it tastes great. No wonder the

222

French have great cooks – great food – great taste. I have found the biggest hurdle is to get out of my old culinary habits. Eat and cook like the French, then you will never be disappointed.

There are always exceptions. We found oven chips. Our oven is super-hot. The two were made for each other like beans and cornbread. We don't eat hot chips in Port Douglas. Our boat oven isn't super-hot so they just don't have that crunch. We found a 1kg bag at *Super U* and made pigs of ourselves over several days. Life is definitely never boring.

Our oven has the unfortunate nickname of the crematorium. It was cheap and doesn't really cut it with thermostatic control. It is either charcoal or pie warmer. After our incinerated chicken affair, I have found cooking requires a bit of inventiveness and a watchful eye. I need to act like a rotisserie, (another French word!).

Although we have a love affair with oven chips it is the pork that is a stand out at the shops. The French go a bundle on pork. Their sausages are just about the best I have tasted on the planet and the chops are fabulous. All this eating necessitates a great deal of walking, otherwise the inevitable would happen. I'd read that 'French women don't get fat'[1]. The quicker I turned French the better.

Naturally, what goes in, must eventually come out.

Every day was a bit of a plumbing lottery.

We managed 22 days. On day 23, just before Christmas, I went down to the grey water sump

---

[1] Mireille Guiliano. Vintage Books London.

for my daily inspection. I didn't like what I saw. We had reached the pipes limit. To use the words choking or gagging just doesn't conjure up the right image. Our drain wallowed in its own inadequacies. I didn't want to be blamed for a cholera outbreak in the village just before Christmas. The kinkmaster hose was pressed into service and we cleared the backlog in the pipe and did a load of washing to flush the sump clean.

So far, the neighbours hadn't seen us burying our unmentionables in the meadow. We hoped to keep it that way.

25

It's only money.

Joy at last. I found our number 50 hidden under a thick growth of ivy. Obviously the Mairie thought it all too hard and gave the Gaelic shrug. Or perhaps they knew something we didn't.

Right after finding our number 50 we found a bill in the post. This was for our habitat tax. We knew all about this particular tax, but the thing that irked us was the injustice. We hadn't actually been living in the house for quite a few months out of the year and they were charging us for the whole caboodle. Surely the French didn't expect us to pay all of it?

I asked Myriam on the likelihood of getting a discounted amount.

'We ask.' Myriam is a 'can do' sort of gal. She offered to take us to the Department of Finances in the nearby village the next day. We could get an answer or pay up. Either way it worked for us.

Naturally the office was closed on a Wednesday.

It was just as well, because we received another bill from the finance department the next day. This must be a mistake. Do the French make mistakes?

On Thursday we waltzed right up to the counter

and Myriam took charge of the situation. I waited, trying to follow the conversation, my credit card at the ready.

The French don't make mistakes when it comes to taxes.

What we had failed to realise in all the paperwork, was that there are 'two' taxes. One for habitat –which is the house and the people living in it, and the other tax for the land.

'Bloody hell,' Boomie said. 'We have 800 square metres of the bloody stuff.'

We began to wish we had bought a caravan on the Costa del Sol.

We had been saving our money to get some cement done under the house. That money slipped over to getting the drains fixed. Now that money would need to go to the Government.

We also found out that if our house is designated our primary residence then the bill would be less.

All we needed to do, (and they say it so glibly) was go to another town, which wasn't serviced by the buses and get a declaration. Not a problem, except you need an appointment. And if we wanted to have our taxes taken out monthly starting in January we should be quick about it. All this one working day before Christmas.

FAT CHANCE!

I had been secretly hoping for snow for Christmas. Now I hoped for a miracle.

I began to panic. Myriam said it wasn't a problem and just threw up her hands. I began to tear my hair out.

'It will happen. I will take you.' We wondered if

we should adopt Myriam, or put her name down for the *Ordre national de la Légion d'honneur.*

Our Christmas day was a quiet affair. Being Sunday *and* Christmas our walk made us feel like we were the only ones left on the planet, except for the woman in the *Boulangerie;* even on Christmas Day the French need fresh bread. We were on a small economy drive and I made pork chops for lunch washed down with a decent champagne… some things are too good to compromise.

Just when we thought we had thrown enough money at the Government our OFII documents finally came in the post. We jumped for joy and cursed at the same time.

Not only did we finally get our medical appointments, we found out how much we had to pay.

There is a very efficient system in France, (a bit of an oxymoron), whereby if you need to pay something to the government the local tabac can help you. They have little pull off stamps of various values. If you have parking fine, you pay for the stamps to the value and then present these when summoned. We had been summoned and needed to pay. Our local tabac man said his wife would collect some stamps for us and we could have them in the afternoon. We wanted quite a lot and they didn't have that many on hand. We duly paid and I carried the envelope home, Boomie acting as shotgun in case of hijack.

We had our future in my backpack and quite a bit of our savings. As our money dwindled, courtesy of the French Government, I wanted the medical before I was bald and had a heart attack.

It's only money

Our appointments in Rennes were scheduled for 9am. We live about an hour by bus to St Brieuc, then about another hour to Rennes by TGV. There was no way we could be there at 9am.

The obvious solution was to change the time. Myriam said she'd ring.

The OFII were having a big lunch.

At 3pm we rang and the answer was

'*No.*'

The only option was to find an Airbnb and overnight in Rennes. More money.

'Impossible. I will take you.' Myriam stepped up to the plate. We'd pay for *gazole*.

'We leave at 6am.'

'*D'accord.*'-

When Myriam says we leave at 6 – we leave at 6.

And while we were spending money like a sailor on shore leave, we had a crack at breaking the bank with some diesel.

Our boiler is of the new variety and runs on *combustable gazole,* a type of diesel. We had been hitting the *gazole* quite hard as we warmed our cockles and the hot water. After a bit of investigation, we asked Howard who he used for fuel. He volunteered to ring for us and came to the rescue with a phone call to the company that delivers.

'*Superbe.*'

We'd be first on the delivery list and that necessitated getting up at the crack of dawn, at 7am for an 8am delivery. It also necessitated having our credit card handy for 500 litres of *combustable gazole,* which doesn't come cheap. If we wanted to be warm we needed to pay.

The truck was on time and in the dark of the early morning I almost gave a Gaelic shrug as I watched our man connect his hose and pour liquid gold into our tank. I had earmarked that money for some renovations. Now it was keeping us warm – which was better than running around in circles or peeling off wallpaper.

We checked our consumption after a week and by a quick reckoning we would need to top up before the end of winter. Oh, how lucky can one person's bank balance be?

26

Bonne année, ★ *Happy New Year.*

New Year's Eve in the norther hemisphere is always a little bit special. Australia is ahead of the game by about ten hours so the internet is awash with good wishes before we, in France, have chilled the champagne.

You can always tell how a country behaves at these sort of celebrations, by what they put in their shopping trolley. We saw booze by the car load, and cakes plus chocolate, a given in the circumstances.

We were out the front surveying our domain on the last day of the year when the previous mayor, Michele came by in his car. He stopped, shook our hands, told us in French that he knew Madame Cansot for about 30 years and held Boomie's hand for an embarrassing long time. Then he invited us to his house should we be around for New Year's Eve. We had only known the man for 20 minutes, but next time we met I would fully expect to have the three Breton kisses. Such is the nature of the French.

The only thing he didn't tell us was where he lived.

Then Myriam came over and invited us to a

party at her house to see in the New Year. We knew where she lived and perhaps it would be a little more fun.

In Australia when one is invited somewhere, it is the custom to bring a plate of food and your particular alcoholic tipple. We had been caught out by the Germans once, when invited over to their boat for drinks. We took our usual contribution only to be admonished severely for bringing anything at all.

'Verboten!'

The French are more laid-back about such things, well Myriam was anyway. She gave a Gaelic shrug – whatever.

Inevitably a friend of Myriam's is a friend of ours. There was a lot of kissing!

Sitting around a table with French speakers is an education. The conversation whips about and in the end all I could do was give up and enjoy the atmosphere. There was also a great many astonishments.

'No!'

'Oui!!

'Impossible!!!'

These and others are accompanied by a gasp and hand signals. High drama.

When two Englishmen, Mike and Bob arrived the French/English ratio was about even and talk came around to Australia.

The tourist board in Australia have a lot to answer for in the way of perceptions. Across the table everyone thought that Australian wildlife was only there to kill you. Poisonous spiders, snakes, crocodiles, jellyfish. It was a persuasive argument for going to Monte Carlo instead.

It was easy to see why we chose our particular village – no crocodiles. The most that happens in the village is a 125cc boy racer comes past the house twice on a Friday night.

The locals had warned us that the Gendarmerie would be out in force for New Year's Eve. We saw two sitting in a car looking at their phones, but I don't think they were pushed to the limit. The Gendarmerie headquarters is usually shut. It never opens on a Monday and has the predictable two-hour lunch. I couldn't see the situation changing for the foreseeable future. Mike was of the same opinion. Our village was a little bit of common sense and decency in an ever-changing world. Here we could bring in the New Year and know it would be like the old year. A year of civility.

Mike and his visitor, Bob lived just around the corner from us and Mike described his house as the one with the turret. Obviously, he couldn't do without one. We'd seen his house on our walks and wondered at the owners of a turret. Now we knew. He was in the process of renovations too and had roped Bob in for some work over the holidays. It helped that they were carpenters and plasterers.

Bob had minimal French, like us, and he found the French a little mystifying. At the pub he asked,

'Un Kroninbourg, *Merci*.'

'*Huh*?'

'Un Kr-o-n-in-bourg, *Merc*i.'

'*Huh?*'

'Un bottle Kron-in-b.o.u.r.g *Merci.*'

'*Ah, Kroninbourg.*'

'It's all in the pronunciation apparently,' Bob said. We sometimes had the same feeling.

What was a surprise about the evening was the choice of music The Breton's have a rich heritage of their own, but it is strongly influenced by the Irish- Celtic traditions. They enjoy Irish bagpipes, clickity clack type dancing and lilting mournful melodies. They are not stuck in the past and when we put on AC/DC everyone sang along like they spoke English from breakfast to suppertime. I was amazed that many of the modern French songs have an intermingling of French/English in the lyrics. But everyone knows how to sing Bohemian Rhapsody by Queen, no matter no-one understands the lyrics.

We also found out a bit more about the Cansots from Myriam's friends.

Louis was a postman and he did his rounds on a bicycle. He died in his 50s and Madame Cansot lived a very long time as a widow. I vaguely wondered how she coped with the drains.

Since our purge with the kinkmaster nothing had poked its head up to greet the New Year. We were being gentle with the plumbing.

'You could always go outside,' I said.

'I am not shitting on the grass like an animal.'

'I could get a pooper scooper.'

'I am not shitting on the grass.'

'I could get some of those little bags and pick it

up and take it to the bin.'

'I am not shitting on the grass.'

You can't please some people.

The next day, while we were in discussion about our drains, Madame from number 7 walked by and began to talk. She spoke a bit of English and we found that Bernadette had done nothing to the house in all the years she was a widow. We could well believe it. Madame, from number 7, knew Bernadette and was glad the house was getting a second go at life. She also offered to give us French lessons, bonus!

The new year would be a good one. Not least because we would finally get our residency permits.

27

A waiting game.

We were four days into the New Year and our drains were behaving. We had been treating them with the upmost care. It was a gamble, but it was paying off. The drain man and his digger were still AWOL, our diverter pipe was taking the strain and we bucketed our washing machine water into the street. It wasn't the best solution, but we had stopped digging holes. Life just ticked along. We visited the library for the internet, such as it was, every day. We went for long walks. I bought a fabulous Aran hand knitted jumper at the Catholics for two Euros and we waited for the day of our medical.

One of our walks took us to a village about an hour away at a good steady pace. This little village had about a dozen houses and a very old church. We meandered around the cemetery looking at old graves when we saw a little area covered with a tiles roof and surrounded by arched windows. On closer inspection it housed the bones of the deceased. The bones obviously came from the old graves. I had catalogued over 200 skeletons in my archaeological days, but the sight of old bones just thrown into a heap in this little area seemed out of the ordinary, no matter it was on consecrated ground. What was interesting to me was the size of the bones. The femurs and skulls were small in comparison to people these days. Bretons through the years were a small people. I could see about a dozen adult individuals and several juveniles in the mix. It brought back all my archaeological digging days as I spotted clavicles, tibias, ribs, fibulas and the rest of the human skeleton. The cemetery had old headstones stacked up at the back of church and we read dates of 1802, 1780 and similar. There was one family plot of significance with a coat of arms and a crown hovering over it. It was at the top of the hill and was at odds to the rest because it wasn't oriented east-west as is traditionally known in Christian burials, but north–south. Whoever they were they were different. It made me think on the permanency of a small village. People living and dying in the same spot for hundreds of years. It was a great way to end a walk in the countryside.

Our village has a multitude of things to do for those inclined to do things. There is Judo, patchwork quilting, oriental dancing and a scrabble club amongst others. They also have a sports club that will teach the intricacies of petanque, that game that looks a lot like carpet bowls. The old folk's home has three courses for petanque. Some houses we have seen on our walks have their own courses. It could be a possibility in the summer months for Boomie, although I think I preferred the oriental dancing.

I was also dabbling in French cake making. Finding the ingredients in the supermarket was an education too.

In France, I had read, supermarkets are not allowed to throw away food. The out of date and tired fruit and veg are discounted to one Euro. One day I picked up a couple of bunches of bananas for a Euro. Having bananas from Guadeloupe and Martinique made me smile. In Port Douglas we lived near the biggest banana farm in Australia. Bananas are as common as mosquitos. Bananas out of season in France are exotic. I made a banana cake and we ate bananas and reminisced of the tropics, while sitting around in slippers and trackie daks.

The other thing we did while we waited was scenarialize on buying another house. Not that we had the money, but dreaming doesn't cost a penny. Our number 5 had been sold, but right in the village square next to the church was number 1. This was an old, old two story house. Built of stone, it fronted right onto the cobbled street. It had been neglected. The yard was bereft of garden, but oh the location, location, location. And it was dirt cheap. Probably because it didn't have much in the way of a bathroom and no hot water system at all. We went into overdrive costing it out. What would it take to make it a great home?

Then there was number 40. This was in much better shape. That was reflected in the price. But the garden needed work. We could do that. We'd done that sort of thing before.

I took a fancy to another number 1 on the hill. This was an old house with a round windows in the attic.

'I've always wanted a round window or two.'

'I know,' Boomie said.

'I could have a writing room in the attic with a

238

round window.'

'I know.' Boomie nodded.

The best bit of number 1 on the hill was the view. It was further up the hill from us and from the patio the whole village and its environs could be seen. I could see myself padding around in slippers, poking the fire, writing in the attic and …

'Living in la la land,' Boomie said. 'We don't have any money for another house.'

'I know.'

Looking at houses at the library on the computers was fun and it distilled our ideas on what we could do with the interior of our little house.

The librarian would look in from her desk as Boomie and I'd cry out,

'Oh no. Oh my God look at that.' Pink tiles in the bathroom and then purple wallpaper to the ceiling. Light fittings that belong in the Adam's Family house. Union Jack wallpaper in the bedroom, including the ceiling. Who in their right mind wallpapers a wardrobe?

We knew we didn't want wallpaper, or pink tiles, or bilious green skirting boards and door frames. And I think I could live without a bathroom that looks like it belonged in an 18th century sanatorium. It was just scary.

The hardware stores have internet sites too and we started to trawl for items we wanted on our wish list. There is nothing like pretending to spend money you don't have.

Our winter rhythm was kicking in nicely and we managed to fill our days doing nothing at all.

At night with the shutter closed against the cold night air we could hear the church bell ringing in the hour, the hoot of an owl and it was peaceful. I could easily conjure up a picture of the Bretons sitting around in winter listening to the crack of the fire, the ticking of the clock. Brittany, and village life stirred my imagination. It was a heady mix that captured me and made me want to stay. It was only in the quiet I heard the drain burp and knew we were living on borrowed time. Even our drain, it seemed, had sensibilities. Perhaps it had performed the Heimlich procedure and dislodged my hose squirter from its epiglottis. I lived in hope, but we seriously doubted our troubles were over.

Doing thing we've never done before is part of the pleasure of being somewhere different. We thought nothing of consuming a block of chocolate in one sitting – an unheard of occurrence in the hot tropics. What we didn't realise was that the chocolate we were buying was cooking chocolate. In Australia cooking chocolate is very much the poor cousin to the real deal. In France cooking chocolate is every bit as delicious as the top shelf. The French always insist on good ingredients. If you wouldn't eat it *au naturel* then why cook with it. I heard someone say the same thing about wine. If you wouldn't drink it – why cook with it. The French do both with aplomb, (Another French word!)

With this in mind I purchased some Tunisian chilli in a tube. *Flame du Cap Bon*. They warn you to be careful. The Ashwins like chilli. We got stuck

240

in and it was delicious. The *piments rouge* were another matter altogether. These little red beauties came with no such warning. They were bloody dynamite and we'd bought a whole jar. The only thing that didn't blow our heads off was the stalks – and only because we didn't eat them.

Out of date cheese should be handled with caution. I grabbed some cheese that looked blue (ish) and nothing special. It was special in that it was really stinky.

'You shouldn't eat something that smells like road kill.'

'But I like it.'

'I'm going to the *la déchetterie* later, I could drop it off if you like.'

'It's quite tasty. It gets better each day.'

'My inner soles smell better than that.'

'It's an acquired taste.'

Boomie wasn't a cheese connoisseur like me.

What we did like was wine. On our last visit we hit the sauce nearly every night so this time we decided in the interest of economy and our liver's wellbeing Friday would be the night when we let our hair down. Letting your hair down is so easy. The alcohol section at *Super U* is well stocked and they always have specials. In our price bracket their reds are tasty, the champagne is very passable, but it is the local pear cider that we grab. *Cidre et Poire* from *Val de Rance* in Cote d'Armor, Brittany is a very tasty drop. They boast on the label it goes well with gormandises and chocolate. Obviously, chocolate isn't considered a food so much as something without which life wouldn't be worth living. I can agree with that. We are not slaves to our tastes and try all manner of drinks. We had yet to find something we can't drink.

All this gormandizing requires some exercise. It was one of those clear cold days that start with a savage frost then turn into glorious sunshine by the afternoon. We had tramped all over the village, but as yet had not been all the way down the Roman road. So we set out and discovered a forest walking track that was just this side of heaven.

There was a stream that followed the track for miles and the two wend their way into natural forest. What is spectacular are the granite outcrops. Huge boulders hug the hillside, some look like they would topple if pushed. Others bigger than a bus and still more the size of a small shed. We walked and began to wonder about the age of these monoliths. We mused they looked perfect for Neolithic dwellers. Brittany is built on Granite. There is even a coastal area called *Côte de Granit Rose*. People have been harvesting the granite for hundreds of years for churches, houses and fences. We saw evidence of this from a large boulder with a neat quarter taken from its side and the marks of the splitting tools still visible. One large grouping resembled a Dolmen. This is two upright stones roofed by a third. With prehistoric monuments all through Brittany it wasn't hard to start putting people in these places and imagining how they lived and died.

Our track meandered around crossing and re-crossing the steam, then the forest gave ground to plantation pine. These huge trees were logged. While they grew their majestic height cut the skyline with dark green.

A very steep climb up a logging track gave us a view of rural Brittany for many kilometres and it was worth the heart pounding effort. Rolling hills covered in trees, forest and plantations for as far as the eye could see. Someone had told us that every bit of France is cultivated and owned by someone. It certainly looked that way from where we were standing.

At the top of the logging track when we stopped to catch our breath and take in the view we met a woman and asked directions and she pointed us back to the village via a stone cross. This was the third 15th century cross marking the village boundaries we had encountered. A task was set to find West.

Crisp, cold air makes a tramp in the countryside a very enjoyable experience. We had walked off a good portion of cakes and chocolate, well, that was the idea anyway, and seen another part of France.

We hoped to see more.

You can't sit around doing nothing, drinking wine, eating cake and not feel a pang of gilt some of the time. When our guilt became an inconvenience, we made plans to get stuck into the garden once more. We had collected quite a heap of cuttings, tree branches and the like and these piles were scattered like compost heaps all over the yard. The thing to do was consolidate our rubbish.

We made a plan, and then on a cold morning, with body warmers and woolly hats we began. The first job was to get rid of the persistent blackberries. These had long tenacious runners which root as they crawl along the ground. We quickly perfected a technique where I would pull and Boomie would grub the roots. They catch on every bit of clothing in a last-ditch effort to hang on, but they were no match for the grubber and my gardening gloves. It took most of the afternoon, but we had made great headway when Boomie said he wanted to move, 'that pile' to 'this pile'. 'That pile' was Cansot rubbish collected over the ages. We began to dig. Old saucepans, ash, old tools including a grubber, hoe and tomahawk all came to the surface. This was the back-yard tip before the dump existed. Old crockery and asbestos, rose bush cuttings, nails, screws and roof tiles all came to the surface as we grubbed, raked and dug. They had delineated the rubbish area with old granite dressed stones and these we grubbed out and kept. They must have weighed around 30kg each. Saving them for later required some effort. Waddling, hugging one of those heavy stones I looked like I was competing for the strongest woman title.

'What are you going to do with them?' Boomie asked.

'Well…I just think we need them.'

'Where?'

'Well…They are too good to just throw away.'

'We don't need more stones.'

'I could put them somewhere until I find where I need them.'

'Women's logic.'

'*Absolument.*'

We also found the biggest worms we had seen so far. On our last trip we found worms. Those were just juniors in comparison. The worms we uncovered were worthy of the Guinness Book of Records. Huge fat monsters. I could see our woodpecker eyeing them off as he watched our racking and digging. The little red robins weren't afraid at all and followed us around snapping up delicious delicacies. They might hate our baguette still hanging in the tree two weeks later, hard as a rock, but they love slugs, snails and worms.

It was while I was bending down pulling and digging I had a bit of a costume failure, as they say on the stage. Because I am in my later years of life, a lot of things have given up and gravity takes its toll. My boobs are a prime example. If I had to give a comparison I would suggest looking at a National Geographic magazine of an African woman in her advanced years digging for roots. I was digging for roots and my boobs slipped right out of their holsters. Of course when you stand up they are all over the place and it's a bit uncomfortable.

'Boomie, I have a problem.' I explained the situation and as Boomie had clean hands and mine were muddy, he did the decent thing and pulled up my jumper and popped the puppies back in. In normal circs this wouldn't be a problem, but at that very moment our neighbour called out a friendly

'*Bonjour!*'

Getting caught with your hands up your wife's jumper is not the sort of impression we wanted to give to our neighbour.

Boomie withdrew and whipped around to return the greeting and caught me fair and square with his elbow in the face. I went down like I'd thrown the fight and landed on a pile of mud and blackberry bushes.

We didn't see the neighbour again. We could just hear her telling her husband all about it. Sexual molestation and domestic violence, right here, in our village.

'*Mon Dieu.*'

Our consolidated pile grew to gigantic proportions. When you are on a roll it's best to keep going. We began to pull the ivy off the plum trees. This wasn't an easy task as the ivy had clung onto the trunk for years and was thick like rope. Louis's resurrected axe took great bites out of the sinewy trunks and I pulled them off. I could almost hear the plum tree sigh with relief as I released it from the strangle hold. The pile of gardening rubbish grew to two metres high. After an Australian half hour lunch we went back to work and tackled the bracken. Bracken is a haven for ticks. I had learnt this when I lived in Britain. I had taken my parents on a nature walk in a forest near Kings Lynn and my mother had come back with about three ticks buried in her neck. I warned Boomie on the tick issue. This pile had been cut a while back and now was dry. Boomie took to the pitchfork like an expert and we cleared the whole area. Then he said we could go inside for a complete examination in case of ticks.

'Later Boomie!'

By the late afternoon we had a mound around three metres by two metres by two metres. Bush turkeys in Australia couldn't match our efforts. The next door neighbour came out to take a look and was rightly impresses. Myriam was amazed. Our neighbour from down the road measured our effort and though we had employed a machine.

The next step would be getting a quote from a local *artisan* to take it all away.

At the end of the day we had a wine and surveyed our domain. It wasn't Shangri-la, but it was our piece of France and just saying it made it feel real. Although it looked like a cross between a paddock and a rubbish heap albeit with bright green patches where the manure was extra rich…

28
Bureaucracy – shmocracy

We had paid our taxes and there was just the small matter of a declaration to say that this was a principal residence in France. No, we didn't have a real estate empire tucked away in a Swiss Bank Account. This little house was it.

So with all our documents in a large folder we bundled into Myriam's car on a cold, blustery, rainy day and made our way across the country to the large town of Guingamp. Here was the seat of Finance for the district. Here we could solve all our problems in one place.

Myriam was a whizz at explaining our situation and the woman on the reception desk listened intently then gave us a number to wait.

We waited.

When called to our interview room the woman once again listened to our little problem.

'We just need to sign something to say that our house is our principal residence in France. Then we could apply for the discounts on offer for our taxes in the future.' We smiled and nodded.

After a consultation with her superior our Madame came back and explained to Myriam.

We needed to apply in Australia for a declaration

to say that this was our principal residence while in France. Then with this stamp, as long as we declare our earnings in France…

The problem we saw straight away was that when we applied for our visa in Sydney we signed a declaration that we wouldn't work in France. I remember the dash in Sydney like it was yesterday. We had no income in France.

Madame frowned.

And there wasn't an overarching authority in Australian that would give us a form to say that we had a principal residence in France.

'We don't have an income in France.'

'But you must.'

'We don't have one.'

Myriam explained the visa issue.

Boomie was worried we might not be paying what we actually owed, because the other tax office had started taking out payments on the precondition that we would get a declaration. He tried to explain his fears.

'You are paying monthly?'

'*Oui.*'

'Then you don't have a problem.'

You can't argue with the logic. We left, not quite sure about anything, but certain that the French tax system would somehow sort it out. They had a year to get it right. And like tax men the world over, they always get their money.

'*D'accord.*'

Just when we thought we could get used to doing nothing, the removalists rang and we arranged to be home for the delivery. Although I had watched every possession go in the box and had written the inventory, it still felt a little like Christmas. To be reunited with our 'stuff' was a happy day. Not least because it all arrived in one piece.

The French men were quick and efficient and within a half hour everything was delivered.

Boomie dived in and we found our new pillows first.

'Goodbye feathers.' He put his pillow on the bed and tried it out.

'Heaven.'

Before we left Australia, we had splashed out on motorcycle jackets and helmets knowing we were going to buy a motorbike and do some continental travelling in the future. I pulled them out and tried everything on. The way to make the dream real is to just go for it. Boomie kitted up and we sat on our kitchen chairs pretending we were biking. It might have been a little idiotic, but it fires the desire to make it all happen.

'Let's be methodical in unpacking,' Boomie said.

'OK.' I knew it wouldn't last. As soon as he opened his tool boxes it would be all over.

I rummaged around and saw my books and reacquainted myself with the titles. These books were from a fabulous second-hand book shop in Port Douglas. I love old travel books. I once read a book on a lady traveller in Egypt and her advice on how to procure a slave for the trip to Thebes. My interest now was Europe. I could do without a slave. I had been boning up on travelling the highway and

250

byways of the continent. Some of my new treasures were from the 1950s. Reading about motorcar vacations in Northern Italy and Southern France in 1952 is entertaining. Reading how to negotiate the roads in Monte Carlo and Lake Como and where to find a good cheap meal are universal themes no matter what century.

'I found my sewing machine.' I pulled it from the box. On our walks I had studied what other people do for curtains and now I could make some of my own.

'I'd forgotten I packed this drill.' Boomie plugged it in and gave it a run.

We had shipped over our printer too and this would make life a whole lot easier dealing with the French and their propensity for copying documents.

I had also packed some of my kitchen implements.

Now we would have plenty to do with all our tools at hand.

Of course, you can't have removals without boxes and when the boxes are empty they need to go to the dump. I could see a dump run coming up.

'And what's the golden rule?'

'Only when you are dumping can you go to the dump shop.' Need I say more!

Getting about a dozen big removal boxes to the dump was a bit of a worry without a car or trailer. This worry was small in comparison to the question of our visas.

'One more sleep,' Boomie said.

The weather had turned nasty overnight and it was a rainy, dull, cold day when we began our journey in Myriam's car to Rennes. Our early appointment for 9am necessitated a dark, 6am start.

'This is it.' Boomie said.

'I know.'

It felt like our whole future depended on our medicals and the French Government. We were healthy specimens, and yet the thought of not getting our visa stamped to say we had the right to stay for the length of our Sydney visa (one year) was always at the back of my mind. This stamp would allow us to follow our dream. After this all we needed to do was apply once a year for a renewal at the local prefecture for the next 5 years then we could get permanent residency. We'd always be Australians, albeit with the bonus of being able to live in France.

Myriam had looked at the weather and it was predicted ice, sleet and a possibility of snow. Just the day to get caught in traffic by the weather. Rennes was only an hour and a half away, but at times we were only doing 40km/h because of the sleet. And it was still dark. We took things predictably slow and still managed to arrive with 30 minutes to spare. Thirty minutes to worry, fret and try to convince myself that the French OFII had this bureaucracy thing all tied up. I also worried that my limited French wouldn't be up to the challenge. Surely the OFII would be bi-lingual. They were dealing with the huddled masses every day.

252

Boomie and I waited at the door for the gong of 9am. Soon there was a gathering of all manner of nationalities waiting for the concierge to open the door. We all clutched our papers, willing everything to be in order.

At precisely 9am the door was unlocked and it was a well-trodden path we followed as we were told to sit and wait. A little window opened and after having our names ticked off, we were given a number. It pays to have an 'A' sometimes as your surname. Boomie and I were top of the list. With our numbers in our hot little hands we went upstairs and waited to be called. The room soon filled and there was a deathly hush, as though talking wasn't allowed. I spotted passports from Madagascar, Saudi Arabia, United States, Senegal and the Philippines.

The first stop was a chest x-ray. The woman radiographer asked me to take everything off from the waist up. That's wasn't a problem, except when I went into the x-ray room she was still mucking about with my passport and papers. Only women can understand about the awkwardness of standing around topless waiting for something to happen. Do you put your hands in your pockets? Do you look like you stand around every day of the week topless in front of strangers? Do you fold your arms? I decided I'd look a bit chilly and went for the folded arms. It was the usual procedure of standing up against the plate and holding your breath. I hadn't had a chest x-ray for about 30 years. I had no idea on the health of my chest. What if they found the black spot? My mind went into overdrive as I thought about having TB.

I went back to the waiting room and Boomie had his turn.

Next was the nurse. She spoke English and was a bright, friendly woman who apologised for taking my blood for a sugar level test. She asked the usual questions, on height, weight and I was sent back to wait for the doctor.

The doctor only spoke French. She spoke very clearly and slowly and I managed most of the conversation talking about my pills, my operations, my inoculations.

She showed me my chest x-ray and explained the large thing on the x-ray was my liver.

'*Grand,*' I said.

'*Oui.*'

Obviously I would need a big liver if I was to live in France. I don't think it was a prerequisite, but it helps.

The last step was the paperwork. When I walked into the office the woman asked, in French, for the things on the list. I was totally prepared and whipped them out. Boomie was ushered in and we handed over our stamps as the final seal on the deal. Giving the money over kinda felt a little sordid. It didn't make us feel like the French actually wanted us, more like the French were willing to take our money. But such is the nature of bureaucracy. There was quite a dossier on the Ashwins on the desk in front of the OFII official. With this last formality we now knew we would be 'in the system'. With a final flourish she stuck our visa stamps in our passports. And that was it.

No muck ups? No last minute dash? This wasn't

what we were accustomed to happening when dealing with the French. It all went like clockwork.

In the corridor we gave each other a high five and walked outside knowing we had achieved what we set out to achieve.

The drive back to our little village was in sunshine and light showers. The gloom had left and it lightened my mood. We would be home in time for lunch, a glass of *Bordeaux,* a few slices of bread and cheese and all the while knowing we were allowed to stay. What a heady feeling.

29

Getting the right information is like pulling teeth.

Euphoria rarely last for long. We had jumped the first two hurdles in our efforts to stay in France as residents. From what we were told, and what I had researched on the internet, the next hurdle- our renewal of our 'titre sejour'- was just a formality.

All we needed to do was go to our local prefecture and re-apply and they would stamp our visa. Easy peasy and we'd be home for lunch.

Thinking ahead is always on my list. With this maxim ringing in our ears we decided we'd just take a trip to our local prefecture and get the low down on what was required, when it was required, and the procedure for acquiring it.

The French, if nothing else are good at handing out forms.

St Brieuc is a sea port with a long history of fishing. They also have Monday off. Most of the shops are shut on a Monday, but the prefecture is open – only from 8.30 to 11.30.

The only bus we could catch was a 6.30am to St B. The other bus would get us in too late. After getting up at 8:30 most mornings 6:30 is a rude awakening. Rural life is like that. If we wanted to live in the sticks, we had to be prepared to take the good with the bad.

This was like a dress rehearsal for the real thing, so our times were a little relaxed. All we wanted was some answers to some knotty questions regarding the procedures of renewal.

We strolled into the prefecture at 9:30 and took a number. All the seats were taken by other hopefuls. We joined the queue of every nationality under the sun and waited.

Some of the hopefuls came out all smiles. Others came out with frowns and one woman was crying. It seemed that the French prefecture had the power of 'a bright future in France' or 'get out and stay out' over someone life. We were the oldest people in line and the only ones with blue eyes. Colonialism has a lot to answer for when it comes to migration.

Our number was blipped on the screen after a good hour and a half wait and we went into a glass room and met a woman who didn't speak any English. That was a good start. With our limited French I explained what we wanted. Our Madame called in a woman who spoke a bit of English.

We went through the Marcel Marceau again and eventually we were all on the same page.

Then, with a wag of her finger, the woman told us that we could only re-apply two months before our visa expired.

The OFII had said three months. The Sydney consulate had said three months. *Here we go again,* I thought.

A quick re-calibration and we thought we could still keep everything under control. Just to be on the safe side we asked the woman to write it all down for us. Not that we would pull the,

'But you said,' card, but it's a useful backup just the same.

We were given our list of documents required and it was more extensive than OFII. This wasn't the walk in the park that I had been led to believe. They even wanted our marriage certificate. I try to think of everything when it comes to the French and so I had brought '*everything*'. Birth certificates, marriage certificates, bank statements, income statements, house documents, the lot. If anyone wanted our life history I had it…plus copies… certified of course!

Naturally they wanted all the documents to be three months old or less. If we could renew at three months instead of two then they would have been current documents. Most of our documents might just scrape in, but some of our banking details and income details would be woefully out of date.

Just another hurdle to overcome. French banking is mired in do this before you do that and don't do that before you do this. Getting a bank statement required us to get our address changed first, as everything was going to Australia and the bank needed our French address. Internet banking for our French bank did include statements, but the prefecture wanted a statement with our address. Who would have thought that the banks email would bounce when I applied to change our address?

'It's lucky we went early to get this sorted.'

'Very lucky.' I had a month up my sleeve.
Game on!

I went to the internet to find out what else we hadn't been told. The woman at the prefecture didn't allude to anything else in the way of surprises. There are a million sights of people living in France and going through the visa issues, renewing visas and enjoying French hospitality once they are legally allowed to stay. My research threw up a few questions I needed to clarify. I found out that in some prefectures after renewal some people would be issued with an ID card and could pick it up… only after their visa expired. Some prefectures issued appointments and others contacted people by letter. Would any of this apply to us? The St B prefecture's web page didn't have any answers. What I needed was someone who could ring and get the information I needed. What we did know for certain was that we needed to pay…with stamps. When it comes to money some things are irrefutable.

What we were after was a timeline on how this thing would pan out. Forewarned is forearmed.

My French wasn't up to the task. I had seen a flyer at the library telling of a woman who could give English lessons. Belinda could ask the right questions in French and get the right answers.

I emailed our interpreter with a list of questions and waited.

Belinda rang the Prefecture and they replied they couldn't answer questions over the phone. Why, I don't know, it was not like we were asking for state secrets. All we wanted to know was the procedure. They did say I could forward an email.

Next Belinda wrote a nicely worded email and we sent it off. After my run with other French officialdom, I wasn't hopeful for an answer.

While we waited life ticked along. We had time to wait, time to get our documents together, time to relax. We had until the 2nd of May.

Having four seasons instead of a tropical two of wet and dry, was a real novelty.

Simple things that we'd taken for granted, like getting the washing dry, were a different experience. One morning Boomie hung out the clothes only to call me about 10minutes later to take a look. All the clothes were frozen on the line.

Boomie held the tablecloth out straight like a magician and his jeans stood up on their own. It was certainly different.

And the temperature dropped to -9 as winter set in. What also dropped was our heating fuel. We calculated that we were using a centimetre a day. If we wanted to keep warm we would need some more. Not a problem if you have oodles of money, but our budget was stretched after our visas, taxes and now more visa money earmarked for the renewal.

So we decided to economise. Boomie turned the thermostat down to 15 degrees in the house and that very night the temperature dropped to -5 degrees and the water froze in our Louis special plumbing pipe. Having a shower in your own soapy soup wasn't much fun. I went out to investigate and when I pulled the pipe apart it was full of ice. The solution was to pull the whole thing to bits, and give them a bash. This was only partially successful. This never happened in the tropics.

I left the pipes in the bright sunshine although the day didn't rise above 0 degrees. It took all day, but the ice eventually came out in one long plug. I felt a bit like a proctologist examining the pipe and its contents. Next was to make sure it didn't happen again. We nutted out a solution which required a brick, a gentle fall, a hose clamp and a test run.

'High five Boomie.'

It seems that you just fix one thing and another goes fffhhhut.

Bernadette, our clock, stopped working. She was wound at 4 o'clock and then decided to stop at 5. We started her again and she gave up at 8. Then for some reason she gave it another go at 8:30 with a half chime. Perhaps she didn't like the cold. It took 24 hours, but she roused herself to carry on, albeit with a chime or two in the middle of the night, just to let us know she was still alive.

The other thing we noticed in the cold was the number of funerals in the town. We had seen two in December and there had been three by the third week of January. These affairs are large. Cars line the main street and all the side streets as people pack the church. The church bells toll the person going in and coming out for the trip to the cemetery up the hill. It is a testament to the number of older residents in the village that funerals are as common as buying a lotto ticket.

Winter, for us was a time to plan what we were going to do, see and renovate. It was also a time to relax. To pass the time Boomie and I continued to walk the village in the cold getting rid of the excesses of chocolate and wine and saw all manner of interesting sights.

The French in our village have either a disregard for their dogs and cats or love them to bits. We have seen dogs with knitted sweaters. Dogs with coats made of blanket material and scarves! Some even take the dog for a walk in a basket and just let it out for the obligatory dump on the footpath. Then there are the dogs that shiver as they live outside…or we assume so as we never see them anywhere else but on the front steps.

There is a small house with two dogs which live outside. One is chained and has a wooden hutch and barks at us every time we go by and his mate is locked in a dark stone outhouse with only his nose poking out from under the door. These two dogs have a hard life. Some weekends we hear gunshots from the forest and barking, shouting and whistling. I can only assume these hardy dogs are working animals. In Australia, working dogs live outside in all weathers. They are bred for it. Hunting dogs in France, I have read, have similar constitutions.

Then there is a dog who lives outside and has the run of the yard and the cat of the same family taunts him from the window. You can almost see the cat thumbing its nose at the dog. It's a comical sight that happens every day. Sometimes the cat will stretch lazily and turn its arse to the dog as if to give the final insult.

We have seen a cat who sits on the outside window sill every day looking in and there is a crazy cat that squeezes itself between the window and the clothes dryer sunning itself. It is like a flat pack cat.

Our neighbour has two little dogs, Gonzo and Pettie Lou. These yappy things are walked twice a day and have gradually become accustomed to us. Apparently Gonzo isn't always in the good books. Sometimes we see him sitting outside on the doormat. Banished for some doggy misdemeanour. The cat mocks him from her perch on the windowsill inside in the sun. He does he penance and then is allowed back inside to sit in the sun on the window ledge, knocking the cat off prime position.

There are also 5 sheep that occupy a small paddock at the side of a house. They look like they have never been sheared. In the cold their woolly coats would be welcome, but they must weigh heavily on their spindly legs. We stop to say *bonjour* and they all run over bleating to stare at us staring at them. It's a regular routine, although they have more stickability than us as we leave the competition early.

But the one animal we really feel sorry for is a chicken. This chicken is lonely, cold and just stands next to the patio window and looks inside. As far as we can see, it rarely moves, and if you look closely you can see all its little peck marks on the window. It so wants to be part of the family. Just down the road is a brood of chickens that live in the lap of luxury, although they would be destined for the pot eventually. They have a dog kennel, a hutch with roosting poles, a great yard for scratching and get all manner of scraps to squabble over. Although one morning there was a flurry of feathers over the yard. Mike, in the turret house, had said his chickens were all taken by a fox. Life and death in the village is never far away.

We have our visiting cat with one cataract. It meows for Boomie every evening and we usually keep a bit of something for it to have a nibble. I'm not sure where it lives, but it's well looked after when it visits us. Boomie bought some treats and now our one-eyed cat comes for its two hour lunch and then dinner at 6.

And we have our fussy birds. They have become so accustomed to us that as soon as we start working in the garden they sit on the fence and wait for the feast of grubs on offer. There are two cheeky red robins who flit about on the ground only a step away from the rake, shovel and mattock. I'm not sure if the worms appreciate being the main meal of the day. At the library there was a pamphlet asking the local population to count birds on a certain weekend and post the results to the census. They have a list, with pictures, and we decided to give it a go. With our boat binoculars we became ornithologists for a day. We had already put out seed for temptation, and managed a decent count of species. What they are called in English besides pigeon, woodpecker and red robin we don't know, but now we do know the French names of our daily visitors.

Because Sunday is a day of doing nothing that requires a power tool, we decided to go for a good decent long walk through the forest. After three consecutive days of below freezing the forest was full of surprises. Our first big surprise was coming across some hunters. Only half an hour into the walk we saw some shooters in the fields. They were decked out in high visibility vests with their guns crooked under their arms. Although we were on the track I wondered if my white pompom on my Aran beanie would be seen. Boomie had his green jacket on which camouflaged him completely. We waved to the shooter and he waved back. A good sign.

Presently a fellow came walking across the field towards us and we waited for him. Best to be standing next to someone who is wearing a high vis vest. He wasn't waiting for us, but the van which trundled up the track behind us.

Then with a blow of his dented, battered looking brass horn which was slung around his neck – a hunting horn that belonged on a tapestry or a dinner service in the Squires lodge – he called up his dogs.

They looked like beagles, about a dozen of them and this man carried a whip to keep them under control. Noses to the ground they swarmed around the pack master. The van door was opened and they piled in, one on top of another.

I asked, '*combien*?' (how many)

'*dix*' (10)

'êtes-vous *de chasse de canard?*' (Are you hunting duck?)

'*Oui.*'

The last to jump in was a female. She came over to us for a sniff. Her whiskers were grey, her udders had seen many a pup and she knew the routine. We watched the dogs jostle for position in the small van.

I asked if he could crack the whip for us. He told us to stand back and with a flourish he whirled the whip above his head and brought it down with a good solid crack that made me jump. Our hunter laughed and the dogs began to bark, but were brought to silence with one word from the driver, and then our man jumped in the van they drove off. A gunshot split the cold air further up the hill.

I had read poaching was a major problem. These men looked like they were having fun. Their dogs certainly were.

We spent a good three hours tramping the forest tracks. The small stream that followed the trail was freely flowing in places, but in the slower margins the ice had formed. Who can't resist throwing a rock to break the ice? We pelted the thick ice, but the rocks skidded off. This stream is tamed only once on its course by a small sluice gate next to a house. The gate was open and the spectacular icicles that formed over the rocks and weeds as the water cascaded, was testament to how cold it had been. The only place the savage frost could not penetrate was the thick carpet of pine needles on the forest floor. The pines had an impenetrable canopy that only thin spears of sunlight could penetrate. The only sounds we heard were woodpeckers, and the faint ringing of the village bell, plus the odd gunshot. It was easy to see how legends and folk tales grow in a landscape of giant granite boulders, soaring oak trees, meandering streams, caves, brambles and weeping rocks.

In some groves where the sun only cast a shadow the ice had grown to carpet everything in geometric designs. Long slender crystals grew on leaves, while other bare branches had a solid clear covering of ice. A thorny gathering of blackberry bushes was covered in tiny ice balls, like someone had scattered sugar frosting over them. Living in the tropics for so long I had an eye for lush, green, wet nature. This was so different, it was magical.

Coming home in bright sunshine to a hot lunch we thought this is what the French do on a Sunday. Although, we'd only met one jogger on our walk, everyone else, if the smoking chimneys were any indication, were sitting inside.

We were expecting the cold, but we didn't count on the sunny days. A clear night meant a beautiful sunny day, albeit cold. The sun brings people outside and the Ashwins were no exception. We decided, while tucked up in bed with a cup of coffee and hot oats, to give the garden a bit of a make-over.

The road to heaven, they say, is paved with good intentions. We didn't get going until after lunch, but we did do something. After a decent half day spent pulling up stuff in the garden and adding it to our pile – in the hope it would still be within the quote re received to take it all away – our next thoughts went to what to plant?

Last May and June the neighbour's gardens were a riot of colour. What we wanted was something that could be kept under control with a line trimmer and something that looked good. In Australia we had bought a reddish plant, we christened the stick plant. This was an outstanding winner as it covered every available space in one season and we could whip it into shape with a trimmer. We looked around for something similar. Not too much to ask. The first place to look for 'what to plant' is the local commune. Our village has a profusion of green verges and spaces. If the commune thought the plant was a good idea, hardy, easy to maintain and pretty then it was good enough for us.

Of course, you can't just go around after dark with a shovel and wheelbarrow, but collecting the odd seed head isn't against the law. We had walked the village enough to know where the 'good stuff' was growing. We also spied what other people did with problem areas ie banks.

The French have in this part of the country a fascination with banks of earth. Properties sometimes don't have a fence, but a large one metre or more bank of earth for separation. Some are planted with a hedge, others have bushes and weed mat and others are just left to their own devices. We have one at the back of our yard which was covered in ivy and Cansot rubbish. When I was digging I found a whole lino floor folded and shovelled into the ground.

We wanted a ground covering not a floor covering and it just so happened that on our walks we passed such a plant.

While Boomie stood look-out I found a small rooted runner and yanked it from its moorings. It's not stealing if it's on the footpath, right?

'Next time we'll bring scissors,' Boomie said.

I planted our ill-gotten gains and we stood back like proud parents looking at our one offspring. It looked like it would go a hundred miles an minute if the parent was any indication.

I'd always wanted a holly tree and as we scoured the yard I found a small one sprouting under the bay tree. I spend ages digging it up and replanting it.

Then I found another and yet more. We had holly trees coming out of our ears.

'We could have a hedge.'

'I'm not having a prickle hedge.'

I could see Boomie's point. We had been trying to divest the garden of prickles in all forms.

'I'll just keep one tree.' I delineated it with some granite rocks I'd dug up and we left it at that.

Until I found an oak tree.

'I've always wanted an oak tree.'

'Knock yourself out,' Boomie said by way of encouragement.

I spend the day digging up a sapling. Who knew they had a tap root that went all the way to Australia. I had a hole about a metre deep before I finally found the end of the root. Then I had to dig a hole the same size to plant it in a different place. I found more Cansot rubbish. A bucket, a fire poker, medicine blister packs and glass perfume bottles. I also discovered sleeping legless lizards deep underground. I picked up one and it gave a lazy yawn and closed his eyes. I reburied him before the robins spied a tasty meal. There was also a nest of spiders all sleeping the winter away underground. And worms, big, fat, juicy worms that didn't seem to have a beginning or end. I sacrificed a few to the birds who couldn't believe their luck to get a meal as big as they were tall.

My oak tree languished for a bit and then died. Not to be outdone I looked for another and after a bit of raking I found about six dozen of the trees. Our neighbour told us to kill, kill, kill. They shed a blanket of leaves and have invasive root systems. It was all the encouragement Boomie needed to go on a killing spree. We needed oak trees like a hole in the head.

'We need shrubs.'

'*Oui.*' I could feel a walk coming on, with scissors.

30
Living is its own reward

Living in a village, getting to know the neighbours, the animals, the daily life of the place made it feel like home.

The days were becoming perceptibly longer and gradually people started to come out of hibernation. On a day when the temperature reached a dizzying 14 we heard a lawnmower. And the garden centre was touting plants. Spring was getting ready to be sprung and it was still a month away.

We slipped into an easy routine and life (as it does) just ticked along.

After travelling on our boat for the last 11 years, moving from here to there and back again it was a grand feeling putting down some permanent roots, albeit in another country. We had plans to travel, but we knew we could always come home.

Of course we still had to sort out our renewal.

Naturally we still had an issue with the drains.

And there was still the matter of sailing to France on our yacht.

'*Absolument*'.
'*Exactement*'.

The photographs

I have no idea who these people may be.

Louis and Bernadette were pointed out to us, but everyone else remains a mystery. Nevertheless, these photographs tell a story which I am happy to share.

French Recipes

I have made all of these recipes many times

I'm the sort of cook that will give most things a try. If I like it then it becomes another favourite to add to my répertoire.

I don't always follow the instructions to the letter as I sometimes just use what is at hand.

Apple biscuit…
Biscuit aux pommes

Which is really a cake, but the French call a lot of their baking biscuits. This is the easiest thing in the world to make because all the ingredients get thrown in at the same time. If I am stewing apples I always pull some out a bit early for this cake (so they don't go all soppy)

4 large apples
45g butter
2 tablespoons Calvados…I used rum (you could miss this altogether if you prefer and just add a bit of stewing juice instead.)
200g all purpose flour (plain)
185g caster sugar (superfine)
1 pinch salt
2 teaspoons cinnamon*
1 teaspoon vanilla essence
2 teaspoons baking powder
90ml orange juice (I just juice one small orange)
155ml peanut oil…(I just use sunflower or canola)
2 eggs
45g almonds on top

*I found cinnamon bark sticks ground by me are *so* much better than the powder on offer. The taste is unbelievable.

Preheat oven 350/180

Grease a 9' or 22cm spongecake tin

Core and slice the apples into 3 slices per quarter.

Melt the butter and brown the apples.

Add the rum and ignite and shake to down the flame.

Remove the apples and drain them so they are not wet.

Put all the other ingredients in a bowl and mix for 1 minute or until it is a smooth batter.

Then layer the apples over a base of the batter. I only do this once, but if you want you can repeat the process ending with the cake batter. Sprinkle with almonds.

Bake for 55 minutes.

Let cool in pan for 5 minutes

Serve warm* with cream.

*It is hard to wait as it smells so delicious.

Walnut cake.
Gâteau aux noix

This cake is the classic nut-loaf. It goes really well spread with butter. It keeps for a long time, but not in our house.

3 eggs
155g caster sugar (superfine)
155g all purpose (plain) flour
60g butter, softened.
200g shelled walnuts. I chop them into small bits or buy them chopped.

Preheat over 400

Put eggs and sugar in a bowl and beat until light in colour.
Stir in flour with spatula
Stir in walnuts and butter
I bake it in a loaf tin.
Bake for 40 minutes. Let cool in pan for 30 minutes
Dust with icing sugar and cinnamon.

Trout with Leek cream sauce
Truites à la crème dé poireaux

The leek cream sauce can be added to anything once you get the hang of it.

30g butter
2 trout cleaned
500g leeks young cut into julienne. Reserve the leaves
2 pinches sugar
2 pinches nutmeg* (I prefer a little less)
Salt and pepper
155g thick crème fraiche (thick cream -dollop type.)

Preheat oven 475

Grease oval dish very lightly with some of the butter.

Wash the trout and steam on a bed of green leek leaves until the fish is cooked. Leave to cool for 3 minutes then remove the skin and put in the greased dish

Melt the butter in a pan

Add leeks and cook, turning often for 8 minutes with the lid just cracked…like steaming.

Add sugar, nutmeg, salt and pepper. Cook uncovered for 2 minutes add cream and bring to boil…only just boiling.

Arrange on top of the fish and pop in the oven for 10 minutes.

*sometimes the French recipes say nutmeg like they invented the stuff. It all depends on your tastes. I try it with nutmeg then if it overpowers the food I leave it out when I make the recipe again.

And to think I only ever used it for rice pudding!

Bacon and onion quiche
Quiche au lard à l'oignon

This is a quiche with a bit more pizazz than bacon and egg pie. I sometimes add a mushroom or a few asparagus*. I use premade pastry, so much easier.
But if you must…

100g all purpose (plain) flour
4 pinches salt
60g butter
1 egg
1tablespoon peanut oil…or canola etc

Mound the flour on a work surface sprinkle salt and make a well. Cut butter into small bits and add to the well with the egg. Knead with finger until it is a dough. Rest in fridge for 15 minutes. Roll out to line a 26cm greased tart pan. Line the pan and then rest dough for 25 minutes.

Filling
1 tablespoon oil
155g bacon thinly sliced
1 onion
45g gruyère cheese grated, or cheddar.
200ml light (single) cream
2 eggs
Salt & pepper.
Put the bacon in the oil and brown. Set aside and then wipe out the pan and brown the onions in the butter

Preheat oven 450

Take pastry shell from fridge and cover the base with the onions and bacon then sprinkle with cheese.

Pour cream into a saucepan and bring just to a simmer.

Beat 2 eggs with a fork in a bowl then add the hot cream and salt, pepper, nutmeg. Pour over the onion and bacon.

Bake for 45 minutes until golden on top and it has risen.

Let it rest for about 10 minutes before trying to cut it….tempting I know, but impossible to cut when hot.

*If you are using asparagus then only canned or really thin young ones can go straight into the mix. Anything a bit fatter will not cook in time. So, I steam some in the microwave for a couple of minutes. If they droop when you lift them then they are probably cooked enough.

Creamed Belgian Endives
Endives à la crème

Endives or Witloof or chicory. The trick is not to cut the bitter inner core into the mix. I used to hate them, until I found out how to cook them with rum.

500g endives
15g butter
Salt
1 teaspoon sugar
2 pinches ground cloves (I use one small pinch)
1 tablespoon lemon juice
1 tablespoon dark rum. -I think this makes the dish!
90ml double cream.

Cut the endive around the core. I cut it from the diagonal turning it around to end with a little cone.
Cook endives in butter for about a minute
Stir in lemon juice
Add rum and cook for 1 minute to get rid of the alcohol
Stir in cream, cover and cook over a low heat for 25 minutes. I sometimes pop it in the oven covered in aluminium foil.

Au Revoir